empty.

*Living Full of Faith
When Life Drains You Dry*

Cherie Hill

© 2012 by Cherie Hill

CONTENTS

BONUS FEATURE:
1st Chapter of
BE STILL (Let Jesus Calm Your Storms)

CONTENTS

BONUS FEATURE:
1st Chapter of
BE STILL (Let Jesus Calm Your Storms)

Dedication

To Jesus,
Thank you for loving me enough
to meet me . . . *at the well*.

Thirsty

Empty. That word pretty much sums it up doesn't it? When life leaves you at a loss for words . . . when you lose your job unexpectedly, when the doctor says cancer is what you're now facing, when your spouse is living life out of control through addictions, when you find out the joy of having a child has now been tainted with "special needs," when your "wayward" child has become completely lost, when your spouse for decades suddenly decides the marriage is over, when financial losses have shattered far too many dreams and driven you into deep despair, when emotional and physical abuse is all you have to wake up to each day, or when death strikes and there are no answers . . . in times like these, there seems to be no words, but "empty" is as close as you'll ever get to describing how you feel.

empty.

Yet, although it's a fitting word, it doesn't even *begin* to explain the condition of the depths of our soul, when we're "empty." Our lives, which are compiled of moments, hours, days, and years, well up from hidden depths within us that reveal more about us than we'd like. It's what's on the surface that gives insight to what's going on within; and at this point, *none of it looks good*. In our desperation, we attempt to fill and satisfy, what we perceive as our deepest needs, but nothing quenches our undying thirst. And "empty" takes on a whole new meaning.

Although the circumstances of our lives seem to aptly define "empty," Webster's definition says that empty is: containing nothing; not occupied or inhabited; lacking reality, substance, meaning, or value; having no purpose. The word seems "well" defined, but in many ways fails, miserably, to fully describe its *true* meaning.

We all find ourselves daily living with the harsh reality that life is *hard* and life *hurts*. We demand that life be fair, yet we're well aware that it's not. Life doesn't waste any time in casting us into the depths of pain through unbearable emptiness; although difficult to imagine, physical pain can sometimes be easier to endure than the ongoing anguish of loneliness, rejection, loss, and failures.

empty.

Pain, physical or emotional, has a way of emptying our soul to the point that we're *certain* we can't go on. And as we plunge into the depths of our soul, we begin to doubt *just about everything.*

Through the emptiness, our soul is *drained dry* and we're not concerned that we'll crack beneath the pressure, we already have. *We find our life being poured out.* And faith seems to be irrelevant as we're scrambling to pick up the pieces of what remains of our so called "personal relationship" with God. If He's so personal, where is He? If He's promised to never leave us nor forsake us, why does it seem as though He has?

When you're empty, you wonder if your faith, up to this point, has meant anything at all. *"Did I ever really believe? Others seem to get it, why can't I?"* With tormenting questions like these flooding our soul, the emptiness only exasperates. The truth is: *we don't like to hurt.* Pain is our enemy—but life has a way of ignoring our desires and forcing us to experience an emptiness that we can't fill. And we'll do *anything* to ease or eliminate the suffering of our soul.

The truth is, we *may have been* living our lives taking God at "His Word," but we find ourselves hardly believing Him, at this point. He seems completely imperceptible by the five senses He's

empty.

given to us. We find ourselves saying something similar to John Updike's characters in *A Month of Sundays,*

"I have not faith.
Or rather, I have faith
but it doesn't seem to apply."

We find ourselves, and our faith, thirsting in greater ways than we ever imagined. Not only are we dehydrated, but there's not even a *mirage* to give us *any* kind of hope.

> *"O God, you are my God;*
> *earnestly I seek you;*
> *my soul* **thirsts** *for you;*
> *my flesh faints for you,*
> *as in a dry and weary land*
> *where there is no water...*
> *my soul clings to you;*
> *your right hand upholds me."*
> Psalm 63:1, 8 (ESV)

This entire Psalm is powerful, indeed, and makes a strong case of how we are to desire God with passionate pursuit. Yet it also suggests that *we will never be satisfied.* We've tried to fill and satisfy what cannot be satisfied by any of our desper-

empty.

ate attempts. In fact, in our efforts to find satisfaction, we have fanned an undying thirst that can't be quenched.

Our faith can take a tragic detour if we overlook this idea of "thirst." While our souls are poured out, emptied by the troubles of this life, we find ourselves *discouraged* by the words of our Savior,

"But whoever drinks of the water
that I shall give him shall never thirst;
but the water that I shall give him
shall be in him a well of water
springing up into everlasting life."
John 4:14 (AKJV)

With every intent to *encourage* us in our faith, in an effort to fill us, we find ourselves emptied even more, as His words haunt our spirit. Jesus said we'd be filled, yet we're *completely*, and *utterly*, *empty*. Doubt begins to make its argument . . . *"God's Word isn't true, He said I'll never thirst, yet I'm empty and thirsting more than I ever imagined possible."* God doesn't appear to be keeping up His end of things. And as life is unraveling, we would expect faith to work. Reasoning within ourselves takes us to a place we never thought we'd be—full

empty.

of unbelief. By all indications, seems like this case is closed and *faith has no defense.*

"When we get our spiritual house in order, we'll be dead. This goes on. You arrive at enough certainty to be able to make your way, but it is making it in darkness. **Don't expect faith to clear things up for you. It is trust, not certainty.***" —*Flannery O'Connor

Why is it that we're thirsty, when Jesus promised we'd never thirst? And if He said we'd never thirst, why are some of *His* last words so resounding throughout history (John 19:28 NIrV):

"I am thirsty."

The One who IS Living Water knows our emptiness, as He takes our sin upon Himself. Sin separates us from God. And there will be a point in our lives, whether by our own wrongdoings or others, where we will fully know the pain of sin. And we will be *thirsty.* We will find ourselves with no strength to carry on.

"My strength is dried up . . ."
Psalm 22:15 (NIV)

empty.

Although what we endure in this life cannot even begin to compare with the suffering of the Cross, we simply can't seem to convince our soul of that. The emptiness that consumes us seems equally comparable. We're thirsty, and we wonder why.

"O God, you are my God, earnestly I seek you;
my soul thirsts for you, my body longs for you,
in a dry and weary land where there is no water."
Psalm 63:1 (NIV)

In our emptiness, we long to be filled, but there are simple elements of faith that seem to get in the way. We can't help but wonder, if we ARE walking in faith, why is it that we're thirsty? Why are we carrying burdens at all? Where is God when our soul is parched in endless desperation? David's Psalm could be our daily journal entry. His thirst, written in Psalm 42, has now become full blown dehydration in Psalm 38, and we can relate:

"I am bent and bowed down greatly;
I go about mourning all the day long.
I am faint and sorely bruised
[deadly cold and quite worn out];
I groan by reason of the disquiet
and moaning of my heart.
My heart throbs, my strength fails me;
as for the light of my eyes, it also is gone from me."
Psalm 38: 6, 8, 10 (AMP)

---

empty.

With the passion of a deer panting for streams of water (Psalm 42:1), our faith plunges us into deeper thirst. Yet, as we thirst, our faith is poured out and we find ourselves believing *"The Faith Lie."*

The Faith Lie

You've heard it . . . you've probably even believed it. You may have bet your faith on it . . . which is why you're empty and hopeless amid the circumstances of your life. It's a little phrase that goes like this:

**"God will never give you more
than you can handle."**

Sounds good. It even seems to give us hope and strength to face one more day, *but it's a lie.* You hear it often—you may even be continually assuring and encouraging yourself through its apparent comfort to your soul. As you face another day of complete emptiness, you find yourself struggling to continually believe that no matter what you face, God is never going to allow you to deal with more than you can handle—that brings reassurance to a spirit that is restless and hopeless. It may

empty.

be what we *want* to hear, but it's not what we NEED to hear. *We need truth.* And the truth is that although this wonderful little phrase has traveled through the generations, leaving a glimpse of hope in its wake, *it's not in the Bible.* God has NEVER said that He won't give us more than we can handle. What He has shown is, throughout history, He ALWAYS gives people MORE than *they* can handle.

"What's the world's greatest lie?" the boy asked.
"It's this: that at a certain point in our lives,
we lose control of what's happening to us,
and our lives become controlled by fate.
That's the world's greatest lie."
—Paulo Coelho

So, where does this lie come from, and how has Truth been twisted? It comes from 1 Corinthians 10:13 (NLT):

"The temptations in your life are no different
from what others experience. And God is faithful.
He will not allow the temptation
to be more than you can stand.
When you are tempted, he will show you a way out
so that you can endure."

---

empty.

We can't be deceived, or our faith will fail—the verse is referring to "temptations," *not* the "troubles" of life. We can look at nearly EVERY situation in the Bible where God shows up in miraculous ways and find that He ALWAYS gave people MORE than they could handle. *That's when God shows up on the scene of people's lives.* Moses didn't part the Red Sea on his own. Daniel should have been devoured in a lion's den. Who survives walking into a fiery furnace? Goliath should have crushed David, and Jonah should have been left for dead. The storm on the Sea of Galilee was obviously going to drown the Disciples, and even Jesus needed help carrying His Cross.

We glean even greater insight into this truth when we look to Paul the Apostle who found himself crushed, beyond his ability to endure. Here's what we learn from Paul in 2 Corinthians 1:8 and the first part of verse 9 (NLT):

*"We were **crushed and overwhelmed beyond our ability to endure**, and we thought we would never live through it. In fact, we expected to die."*

Hardly seems like a loving God would allow such saints to go through such anguish, but our faulty thinking is simply because we don't understand His ways. It is out of His great love for them

empty.

that He allowed them to face the impossible. Why is that? It's because of the *second* part of verse 9 from 2 Corinthians (NLT):

*"But as a result, **we stopped relying on ourselves and learned to rely only on God**, who raises the dead."*

There's purpose through the pain, there's a reason for our emptiness. God ALWAYS gives us more than we can handle, in order to reveal what *He* is able to do through our faith in Him. We must be emptied of ourselves, so that God Himself can fill us—He wants to show us that prayer works. He wants to bring about miracles that go far beyond our imagination. He wants to display His power, presence, and glory. Without situations in life that we CAN'T handle, we'd never need God to show up. Why would we even need to pray at all? We'd never have the opportunity to see *our own Red Seas* parted. Who wants to miss out on that??

It's critical to the survival of your faith that you stop believing the lie. Here's the truth:

If God is only giving you what you CAN handle,

you're not learning to depend upon God,
you're not stepping out in faith,
and your faith isn't growing.

empty.

In fact, if you're facing situations that are far beyond your control . . . God is trusting you more than you trust Him. He obviously knows that He's given you a measure of faith that is much more than you think. We need to clearly understand that faith is a journey that involves overwhelming disappointments, joys and sorrows, periods of waiting, and plain and simple long suffering that gives no evidence that it will ever end. The truth is, no matter how much we prepare, take precautions, and try to eliminate risks in life, we'll never succeed. *And faith is hard.* Don't let the lies about faith cause you to turn away from God, or worse yet, remake Him in your own image.

If we'll leave the lie behind and move on in greater faith, knowing that every obstacle is an opportunity for faith to rise above it, we'll find ourselves experiencing the peace that God promises to give us as we trust in Him. If Jesus emptied Himself, shouldn't we also see it as a necessary part of our faith, instead of viewing it as God's greatest failure in our lives?

"Have this mind among yourselves,
which is yours in Christ Jesus, who,
though he was in the form of God,
did not count equality with God a thing to be

empty.

*grasped, but **emptied himself**, by taking the form of a*
servant, being born in the likeness of men.
And being found in human form, he humbled himself
by becoming obedient to the point of death,
even death on a cross."
Philippians 2:5-8 (ESV)

God's goal: to bring us to a place where we realize we can't do it without Him. It's about bringing us to the Cross—as many times as it takes, so that our relationship with Him is the wellspring of our lives. Our place of emptiness is exactly where He needs us, in order that we might fully realize that our need for Him is greater than any other. (And all too often we need to be reminded of that.) If you're empty, you can be sure you're about to be filled. But first, you must clearly understand *why* it is you're thirsty. You need to take a look at the *emptiness* and grasp the *fullness* of its purpose.

Empty

Before we can be filled, we need to grasp the full meaning of our emptiness. Our God speaks directly to us regarding our emptiness. He tells us, without hesitation, *why* we're empty in Jeremiah 2:13 (NIV):

empty.

"My people have committed two sins:
They have forsaken me, the spring of living water,
and have dug their own cisterns,
broken cisterns that cannot hold water."

What's a cistern? We certainly didn't know we dug one and we definitely didn't realize it was broken! The definition by Webster gives us clear meaning: an *artificial reservoir* for storing liquids, especially water (italics mine). Confusion gets the best of us as we try, desperately, to understand our emptiness. But there's no need for confusion, we've simply misunderstood the purpose of our lives; and in order to be filled, we *need* to be poured out . . . because sin, our faulty thinking, our idea that being "empty" is contrary to God's best in our lives, *keeps us from being filled.* And here's where we get a clear understanding of emptiness.

We're empty because we're more concerned about "feeling" better than finding God. We struggle because the sinful nature within us tells us that God exists for us, not that we exist for Him. And that's normal—that's our fallen human nature. And life has a way of tainting the Truth. The troubles of this world are so overwhelming that it's difficult at best to even *consider* "living for

empty.

God" and His purposes, when we're consumed with needs that seem even greater than what God can meet.

Life seems to have a way of throwing us into such confusion and pain that we simply lose *all* hope—our joy is gone and nothing encourages us. We're forced to face a truth we just can't grasp: we can live obediently, believe God, practice our spiritual disciplines, walk in the fullness of Christ, but troubles still come . . . and we still find ourselves *empty*. We're continually assured that we cannot escape this life, which seems like endless pain and problems. We can find ourselves being poured out, even in our yearning to be filled.

Through our daily struggles, we grasp the fact that simply "walking by faith," following God's plan, isn't enough. It seems clear that even if we apply Biblical principles, we don't always get what we want. *That's not the way we hoped faith worked.*

What we really want through unpredictable struggles is someone we can trust. We want hope, joy, and peace amid all the uncertainty, pain, and endless confusion. And without someone we can trust through it all, we do one of two things: We either pretend things are better than they really are or we find a way to relieve the pain. When we

empty.

look at our troubles, we see them as senseless and meaningless. The randomness of life seems to give evidence that *God may very well not even exist at all.*

When we can't find God in the emptiness of our souls, we tend to throw up defense mechanisms that keep us from being thrown into an abyss. We deny how much we struggle and hurt, we ignore our unanswerable questions and we keep telling ourselves that everything will be alright. We stand firm in our faith, from all outward appearances, declaring our love for Jesus, our love for others, and even profess to be finding our supply of strength from streams of Living Water. And yet, we feel that if we were to hear, "Just trust God," one more time, we might just be emptied enough *to never want to be filled.* In a moment of truth, when we're consumed with relieving the pain behind our problems, we must come to grips with the fact that Christianity offers no simple formula for making life work the way we want it to. We want solutions to our problems, instead of a pathway to God. We disguise our selfish desires for temporary relief rather than allowing that pain, emptiness, to be the very thing that shows us that something inside of us is desperately wrong.

We create our own obstacles to God. And if we only evaluate God by what we see and feel, we

empty.

will continue to look to ourselves, loving and clinging to our lives, with all our heart and soul, instead of to God.

As we struggle through our emptiness, another lie seeps into our soul's reasoning, when we so wrongfully believe that if only God would show up, we'd *feel* better and our troubles would disappear. But *finding God has never been about finding Him.* He's always been there. We're assured that if we look for Him, we'll find Him. So that's not the point.

"You will seek me and find me."
Jeremiah 29:13 (ESV)

It's when we find God that we find ourselves. It's in developing a passion to know Him that we are filled. And until we are filled with a passion to know Him in greater ways than we know Him at this very moment, we will never view our emptiness as an opportunity to experience God in greater ways than we could ever imagine. It's in understanding the depths of our emptiness that we learn *where to go* to be filled. But, too often we're consumed with the reality of our emptiness and *we're unable to get to God.*

When emptiness descends upon us, our soul can cry out in gut-wrenching pain; unspeakable,

empty.

unthinkable pain. We find ourselves unable to endure what we know to be true: *life is painful and nothing satisfies.* We find no relief, nothing is certain, there is no rest, and our greatest joys have been far outweighed by our present sorrows. We struggle down far too many paths that all lead back to ourselves, and we're unable to find our way to God. We plead and hope for God to speak, but in a moment when we need Him most, there is nothing. Silence. We find ourselves beyond the reach of anyone but God and we're suddenly faced with an emptiness that we never thought possible because *we can't even find Him.*

As we pause for a moment and take a look at our lives, we realize that we *have* dug our own cistern, and *clearly* it is broken. We become consumed with supplying our own souls, arranging our lives around meeting our needs, instead of allowing God to fill us with *His* fullness.

We're passionately pursuing everything but Him alone, and we find ourselves . . . *empty.*

> *"Whoever seeks to preserve his life will lose it,*
> *but whoever loses his life will keep it."*
> Luke 17:33 (ESV)

If we apply this to our poured out lives, we find that it reads, *"Empty yourself and you'll be filled."*

empty.

Seems simple enough—but there's *nothing* simple about it. We find our souls in twisted frustration because emptying ourselves is contrary to our two primary goals in life: (1) find a way to achieve happiness and (2) influence and manipulate people and their resources to cooperate with achieving that goal. Even as Christians, we claim heaven as our home, immigrants in a foreign land, but we live like we're natives to the earth. It seems an impossible feat to have a passion for something other than our immediate satisfaction—our temporary desires matter far more than God's glory. We work feverishly to fill ourselves and only end up emptier.

We dig our own cisterns because we know that life is overwhelming and intolerable and that truth is simply too painful to admit. We'd rather lie to ourselves and dig our own wells, than to admit to the terrifying truth that we desperately need God—a God who seems more absent than present.

Our emptiness brings us to the end of ourselves. And it's in our emptiness that we learn that our deepest desires are inconsolable.

"If I find myself in a desire in which no experience in this world can satisfy, the most probable explanation is that I was made for another world."—C.S. Lewis

empty.

We're thirsty for a reason. We are empty, so that we will have the need to draw water. Our emptiness comes from God. Nothing in this life will satisfy. Try as we might, we continually wake up and look in the mirror, only to find ourselves resembling this guy:

Insatiable—always thirsty, never satisfied. God was right, we've dug our own cisterns and they *are* broken. And it's important that we understand the cistern, because God wants to show us something. He wants to meet with us, face to face, one on one, but we need to have a full understanding of our current condition.

We're empty because *we're using a cistern*. A cistern is a container that comes in various shapes and sizes around the world. They are used for the purpose of *storing* water, both above and below ground, but it can't do what a "well" does. A well

empty.

taps into a supply of groundwater, like a spring or underground stream. If you know anything about wells, they are built by digging into the earth and inserting reinforcements, so that the interior walls of the well do not collapse.

Wells have been used for centuries and historically people have taken advantage of natural springs and built their settlements near them. People could easily access the water by lowering their buckets, filling them, and pulling them up. Whenever they needed water, *they would go to the well.*

Cisterns, on the other hand, are designed to *store* water, not tap into an existing, continual water source. Cisterns were primarily used for collecting rain water—not the same as spring water, mind you. And historically, cisterns were used in dry regions to store water, in the event that a well failed or rainfall ceased. People used them as a *backup* water supply. With a cistern, *someone has to fill it* with water. They aren't wells, which provide a *constant* "source" of water.

So, what does this have to do with our emptiness in life? A lot. We continually use cisterns to satisfy our thirst, God wants us coming to Him, The Well. We try to contain our happiness and joy within the things of this world, but we're in a dry

empty.

region, a sinful one. And God knows that our cisterns will fail to be filled, or worse, simply crack and be rendered useless from being dried out. We fill our cisterns (bank accounts) with money and they run out . . . then begins the endless cycle of having to fill them again. We fill our hearts with relationships which help us *feel* loved . . . and people hurt us. We try to dull our pain by filling new cisterns of alcohol and drugs, or by consuming our time with useless things in an effort to find temporary relief from the reality that the cistern is not supplying the demands of our "needs"—it has to *continually* be filled. We're exhausted from the endless job of filling it and we're left *empty*.

Our emptiness directs us to The Well, God Himself. It's in accepting our emptiness that we can understand how "being thirsty" helps us to grasp that nothing we can do or experience in this world will ever satisfy us with what our soul yearns for most—we want to be filled . . . in a way that we are satisfied, *completely*. Our greatest desire is to *never be thirsty again*.

But our ways are hardly ever like God's. We need to meet with God over this matter. We need Him to speak to us and break His silence. But, before we meet God, face to face, we need to understand more clearly how it is He works, when it

empty.

comes to emptiness. We need to understand *"The Empty Principle."*

The Empty Principle

Too often, we get it all wrong in life. We assume that God works the way *we* think He should and we set ourselves up for mammoth disappointments. God's ways are not our ways (Isaiah 55:8)—the sooner we accept that, the better off we'll be. When it comes to emptiness, once again, *we get it wrong.*

In our daily life, we endlessly strive to preserve what is precious and end up losing it all *and* more. We tend to believe that if we're empty, we have nothing left. And that is certainly true if we're not connected to God and living out His purposes for our lives. But, if we're walking in faith, believing His Promises, trusting in Him fully, then He is going to REQUIRE that we're empty, so that He can fill us and we can be poured out. Huh? God's way in "emptiness" is this: *The more you pour out, the more there is to pour out.* Put another way: *The emptier we are, the more we can be filled.* Ahhh, that's better. But it still doesn't make much sense. We think this through and can't help but reason that if we're

empty.

"empty," we have nothing left . . . right? Wrong.

We'll need to go to 2 Kings 4 in the Bible and take a look at this principle . . . *"The Empty Principle."* The whole thing starts with Elijah going to heaven. Evidently, the sons of the prophets were watching as a chariot of fire came down and took him. And there was a woman who was the wife of one of the sons of the prophets . . . who died in the whole event.

So, this widow, goes to Elisha (don't confuse him with Elijah—not one in the same), and tells him that she has nothing left, her husband's creditors are coming after her and they are coming to take her two sons away from her to be slaves (2 Kings 4:4). So, Elisha asks her what she has in her home and she tells him she only has one jar of olive oil. In her mind, life is over—she's empty in more ways than she can count. But, through *"The Empty Principle,"* she's got more than enough. Here's what happens:

3 Elisha said, *"Go around and ask all your neighbors for empty jars. Don't ask for just a few.* 4 *Then go inside and shut the door behind you and your sons. Pour oil into all the jars, and as each is filled, put it to one side."*

5 She left him and shut the door behind her and her sons. They brought the jars to her and she kept

empty.

pouring. ⁶When all the jars were full, she said to her son, *"Bring me another one."*

But he replied, *"There is not a jar left."* Then the oil stopped flowing.

⁷She went and told the man of God, and he said, *"Go, sell the oil and pay your debts. You and your sons can live on what is left."*

A miracle. The most famous last words before God shows up are: *"I have nothing."* Put many other ways: *"I can't go on. My pain is too deep. I'm empty."* We need to grasp this principle. It's vital. We'll never be filled until we do. Here's the promise through *"The Empty Principle"*: When God is your Source, there is *never* a shortage. Through this woman's emptiness, we're shown a remarkable miracle and a profound spiritual principle.

We believe that we need to be filled in order for God to use us, but God is looking for those who are *empty*. If we're empty, *we can be filled.* It's actually quite simple. We look at the widow and see that as long as there was something "empty" that could be filled in the widow's home, the oil didn't stop flowing. As long as *we're* empty, God can flow through us. Grasp this truth: Emptiness is not the end, *it's the beginning.*

empty.

We can understand this principle even further as we grasp the point of this miracle: As long as God has empty vessels, people who are wholly yielded to Him, He pours out His Spirit without measure.

> "... *for God gives the Spirit without limit.*"
> John 3:34 (NIV)

But, when the vessels have been filled, they must be poured out. If God seems to be emptying your life, removing just about everything you count on and hold dear, you can be sure He's at work ... *He's about to dig a well in your soul.*

If we're the ones filling ourselves, with the passions of this world, we can't be filled by God—we're doing the digging *and* the filling, *not God.* And we'll work endlessly to keep filling because we'll never be satisfied . . . and we can't live on "empty." But, everything we fill ourselves with dulls our ability and desire to be filled by God. Instead of seeing our emptiness as the end, we need to start seeing it as the greatest opportunity to be filled by God Himself. Our problem is that we tend to feel as though we should be filled *before* we can be poured out—***God wants us empty.***

It's in our emptiness that we will be filled by His Spirit . . . to experience a fullness that we have

empty.

never imagined. What we learn through this principle is that when you rely in faith on God's provision as your Source, there is never a shortage. It's an internal "well" that just continues to pour into you as you pour it out. So, if we're thirsty, it simply means we're not being poured out. *Although, we'd gladly argue endlessly over that point.* It's through *"The Empty Principle"* that we learn . . . as long as we are empty vessels, who are wholly yielded to God, He pours out His Spirit into us and we will overflow like rivers of living water.

"Whoever believes in me, as Scripture has said,
rivers of living water will flow from within them."
John 7:38 (NIV)

And here's the sad truth: far too many believers have the Holy Spirit *dwelling inside* of them, but *not flowing out* of them. We need to deeply understand *"The Empty Principle."* And we need to fully comprehend that we need to go to the Source that will *truly* satisfy. Even Job knew this great need and he knew he had to go to the Source—Job 23:3 (NIV):

"If only I knew where to find God,
I would go to his dwelling."

empty.

When we're thirsty, there's something we need, desperately. But, it's not what we think. What we thirst for doesn't even compare with what God wants to give us. Our prayers fall far short of God's best in our lives. He wants to give us so much more than we ever ask for (Ephesians 3:20) ... and most of the time He does, even when we least deserve it—*that's His grace.*

So, we hear His promises, we long for all that He gives . . . the FULLNESS of life. We know what Jesus has said,

"Everyone who drinks this water will be thirsty again, but whoever drinks the water I give them will never thirst. Indeed, the water I give them will become in them a spring of water welling up to eternal life."
John 4:13-14 (NIV)

and we realize that *Jesus* has what we need. He offers what will quench our undying thirst, and we find ourselves repeating the wise words of a woman who was just as thirsty as we are:

"Give me this water
*so that I won't get thirsty
and have to keep coming here to draw water."*
John 4:15 (NIV)

---

empty.

You're ready to be filled. You desperately want your thirst satisfied, so that you will never thirst again, but you look for God and can't seem to find Him, anywhere. Yet, you need to look no further ... *He's been waiting for you.* He wants to meet with you, one on one . . . *at the well.*

empty.

At the Well

You may not have ever realized this before, but *your* story is written *somewhere* in the Bible. Your name could be written in, in the place of any one of the biblical characters you read about. Although the story may not be *identical*, there are always parts of a story that are a replica of your own. Chances are, you have lived out, not just one, but multiple stories within the Bible.

Your life is writing a story, and when you're empty, you need to know one thing: If you're allowing God to be the author and perfecter of your faith, which He clearly says He is (Hebrews 12:2), then *this life is not the end of the story*. And that explains a lot. It explains why Christians suffer through pain and sorrow and are all too often rejected by the world. It helps us to make sense of why God doesn't fulfill some of His promises here on earth. It gives us insight into why prayers go

empty.

seemingly unanswered and life is relentlessly unfair. Our life's story, as believers in Christ as Savior, doesn't end at death—death is only the beginning. But, while we're here, our story is being written. How it ends is up to us. Throughout this life we face test after test; and worse yet, we tend to more frequently encounter the dreaded "pop quiz." Our story will entail challenges to trust God in ways we never imagined we could, or would, and we'll one day realize that this was all temporary—this story, our life doesn't define us in eternity, but it prepares us for it. Our "name" doesn't matter, our permanent home after we end the story of our life does.

Interestingly, there's an account in the Bible where a woman, who has a personal one on one account with Jesus, gives no mention of her name. Quite possibly her name could be yours. And you'll recognize yourself in her words and in her person, as *you* go to the well.

It has been said that of all the physical human needs that we can feel, none is more intense as the want of water. *We were meant to thirst*, but not for the things we dig our own wells for. Our soul thirsts in a desperate desire for the water of Life. The thirst thrusts us into action to satisfy it. Yet, we only find ourselves thirsting more and more.

empty.

Our wells provide a water that is utterly power-less to quench our thirsty soul—like drinking sea water, we become only more parched and thirsty as we drink.

The poet, Samuel Taylor Coleridge expressed this dire situation in his 1798 poem entitled, "The Rime of the Ancient Mariner":

Day after day, day after day,
We stuck, nor breath nor motion;
As idle as a painted ship
Upon a painted ocean.

Water, water, every where,
And all the boards did shrink;
Water, water, every where,
Nor any drop to drink.

Nothing could describe our situation more accu-rately. The pain of unsatisfied desires of the soul hardly need mentioning; in fact, we'd rather not reveal them: longings, desires, hopes—both physi-cally and spiritually. We thirst for power, pleas-ure, money, respect, love, and wisdom . . . it's an infinite list. We look for what our spirits need in a physical world that cannot supply it. We need to understand our thirst. No one goes to the Well, *unless they are thirsty.*

empty.

Thirst brought a woman out of Samaria to a well . . . *where she met Jesus.* At that well, her life was transformed in unforeseen ways—forever. Our lives will be too, *that's what happens when you get one on one with Jesus.*

Weary

There's a place we all come to before we go to the Well. It's that desperate place where we have no strength to carry on . . . we're weary—exhausted from our efforts to satisfy our undying thirst. In John 4:6 (NIV), we find Jesus at a place of weariness from his travels:

> *". . . Jesus tired as he was from the journey,*
> *sat down by the well."*

Jesus, being fully God and *fully man*, suffered from physical limitations, as we do. And He went to a well, but not just *any* well. Jesus had a Divine appointment with a woman, just as He has a divine appointment with each of us. (It's up to us whether or not we make the appointment . . . some of us show up, but a little late. Never mind, Jesus will wait.) Jesus chose to leave Judea (Judea had its own wishes, ways, and desires.) and go to Galilee,

empty.

where there were fewer prejudices and more open minds. It was a choice place where He could get His kingdom well rooted before He returned to Judea.

So Jesus went by way of the great highways leading to a valley into a city called Sychar. It was a city that Jacob gave to his son Joseph (Gen. 33:18-20; 48:22). There are very few places in Palestine, after Jerusalem, that have more biblical historical events connected to them as Sychar. There is no spot in all of the Holy Land that is more attractive and richer in biblical associations . . . and Jesus overlooked it all, as He sat down to rest by the well.

Jacob's well, where Jesus sat, is one of the few sites that is spoken of biblically where there is absolutely no dispute. It is a half mile south of Askar, and a mile from Nablus. The well is 75 feet deep, but was originally much deeper. The well is about 7 feet, 6 inches in diameter, yet the mouth of it is only 4 feet wide—only large enough for a man to pass through with arms uplifted. There is no mention of Jacob actually digging a well, so no one is certain of its origin. Nevertheless, the well is there. Truly, it is one of the few authentic places that is identified as a "place where Jesus sat."

The woman from Samaria had no idea what

empty.

she was in for that day. God's mercy is new every morning (Lamentations 3:22-24) *and full of surprises.* And soon, she would fully realize Lamentations 24 . . . *the Lord became her portion.* Jesus knew her need before she did. And He knows your needs as well. To us, it may seem that God is full of surprises, but they are no surprise to Him. Every detail happens just as He planned all along. When it comes to God, it's all about Divine appointments. His ways are not haphazard. They are meticulously orchestrated; timing is crucial for His perfect plans to unfold. And everything plays out on a schedule that is managed by His divine clock (John 7:30, 8:20, 13:1).

Timing was critical when it came to this Divine appointment at the well, too. When God moves, He moves strategically and He knows every facet of a situation that must come together to complete His perfect plan. Here's the thing: The route Jesus took to Samaria is not the only route between Judea and Galilee. In fact, the path He took was the least common one, yet the most direct one.

Due to the Jewish hostilities toward the Samaritan people, the Hebrews most frequently would travel to the east; crossing over the Jordan, and thereby avoiding the Samaritan territory. Skirting Samaria was a detour that would take much long-

empty.

er than the normal three days of travel. Jesus, however, didn't hesitate to travel through Samaritan territory (Luke 9:51-56; 17:11-19; John 4:1). Jesus took this route for no other reason than that He had a "Divine appointment." Jesus' purpose on earth was continually guided by situations where He was needed in a Divine way (Luke 2:49; 4:43; 19:5; 24:7; John 9:4; 10:16; 20:9). In this case, He went out of His way, in His weariness, to meet a woman who desperately needed Him. He wasn't concerned with the prejudices that caused others to take a detour around the city—He was on a mission, an eternal one. *He had a well to dig.*

Having walked for days, Jesus came to the well and sat down. The time for His appointment had arrived. So He waited.

". . . Jesus, tired as he was from the journey, sat down by the well. It was about noon." (John 4:6 NIV)

High noon. The sun was directly beating down. We can assume it was a time of day when one's thirst peaks. Yet, sitting by the well, *He waits.* He doesn't ask the disciples to draw water for Him (He sends them into town to buy food), or draw it Himself, he waits . . . on a Samaritan woman. And the conversation that took place is the longest one

empty.

on one conversation with Jesus that is recorded in Scripture.

One On One With Jesus

Jesus made it clear throughout His ministry on earth that He didn't like rules. The God of the Ten Commandments tossed out religious rules, *religiously*. This time, at the well, He decided to toss out all kinds of rules: (1) Jews weren't supposed to speak to Samaritans. (2) Men weren't permitted to address women without their husbands present. And (3) Rabbis shouldn't talk to a woman of this one's character.

Without hesitation, Jesus breaks all the rules with one simple, short question:

"Will you give me a drink?"
John 4:7 (NIV)

Even the woman responds in shock, reminding Him that He's breaking the rules:

"You are a Jew and I am a Samaritan woman.
How can you ask me for a drink?"
John 4:8 (NIV)

empty.

But Jesus pays no attention to the rules. His purposes go far beyond them. First, and foremost, He starts His one on one time with the woman by introducing her to *"The Empty Principle."* You remember it don't you? And here we see Jesus laying it out. Before the woman knows her need, before she fully understands the depths of her *true* emptiness, *Jesus asks her for something.* He asks her to take what she has and ***pour it out* for Him.**

What she thirsted for wasn't water, but something more, something deeper that her soul so desperately yearned for . . . a *personal* and *intimate* relationship with God.

Presbyterian theologian R.C. Sproul was asked, *"What do you think is the greatest spiritual need in the world today?"* And He answered, *"The greatest spiritual need in the world today is that people need to discover the true identity of God."*

It's this one on one appointment with this woman from Samaria that we see Jesus point out her greatest need . . . to know His true identity. He asks the most important question that He also asks us, *"Do you know who you're speaking to?"* When you're praying, crying out to the heavens, do you fully understand who it is you're calling to?

empty.

"If you had only known and had recognized God's gift and Who this is that is saying to you, Give Me a drink, you would have asked Him [instead] and He would have given you living water."
John 4:10 (NIV)

In this woman's emptiness, she came to a well, to draw water, and her life has just taken one of the most confusing turns imaginable. She just came to the well for water—now she's faced with a Jew breaking all the religious/social rules, casting her life into the deep, before she even realizes what's happening.

And she does what we all do when we meet one on one with Jesus and He asks us to open up our hearts and offer Him something from our lives . . . *we make excuses.* In fact, she even questions Jesus' authority—who He is. Don't we do the same? *How is it that this God we cannot see asks so much of us? How are we to trust someone that has not plainly made Himself visible? How can we sacrifice anything of our lives to Him when He won't even show His face?* As we listen to the words of the woman, we can relate:

"But sir, you don't have a rope or a bucket," she said, "and this well is very deep. Where would you get this

empty.

living water? And besides, do you think you're greater than our ancestor Jacob, who gave us this well? How can you offer better water than he and his sons and his animals enjoyed?" (John 4: 11-12 NIV)

We know she's talking to Jesus!—*she* doesn't. She turns from being shocked by Jesus' words and actions, to being appalled by what He's asked her to do. We're no different. In essence, she's telling Jesus, "Why don't you do it yourself!" "You want me to use what *I* have to help *you?*" "Who do you think you are that the resources you offer me are any greater than the greatest persons to live the earth?" "How can you offer anything better than what the world can?"

Tough questions. *But not for God.* He knows how to handle our doubt, disbelief, and sin. And in His usual way, Jesus skirts the meaningless issues and gets to the heart of the whole appointment. He came to draw water, but what He's doing, at this point, is drawing her soul to Himself. And the words He spoke to her resound throughout history:

> *"Anyone who drinks this water*
> *will soon become thirsty again.*
> *But those who drink the water*
> *I give will never be thirsty again.*

---

empty.

It becomes a fresh, bubbling spring within them,
giving them eternal life."
John 4: 13-14 (NIV)

We can only imagine the confusion upon her face. We too are confused. We go to God with our unmet needs, pleading out of desperation for our Savior to save us from the troubles of this life and we get something *entirely* different. We call out to Him to take down our enemies and He tells us to love them. We ask for financial help and He tells us to freely give. We plead for His presence and He answers us with His silence. And we wonder, *"Did God not hear me right?"* Did I somehow not communicate well? What doesn't He get? Doesn't He see that I have NOTHING to give?? If He supposedly sees "the big picture," He sure isn't paying attention to it!

And yet, even through this woman's confusion, it's clear that Jesus has grabbed hold of her soul. Something has resonated. He has drawn her in by her thirst and then promises to alleviate her constant need to draw water, *forever.* She knows that what He's said goes far beyond the surface of her soul, as His words have penetrated the depths of her spirit and she clings to the key words, *"whoever drinks the water I give him **will never thirst.**"*

empty.

Those words grab hold of us as well, as we sit here at the well with Jesus. We're thirsty and nothing satisfies. We come to the well we've dug, over and over, and we're weary; we've come to the point where we've lost the strength to even draw from it. *It doesn't get worse than that.* We're tired of what keeps us digging wells that never satisfy . . . the thoughts of: If I just had more money, more friends, more love, more success, more excitement, a better job, a better husband/wife, a better education, a closer family, a little more time, a better church . . . *then,* I would be satisfied. We're so eager to satisfy our physical, temporary desires, that we overlook our more important *spiritual* ones.

But, deep down, we know those present things, those temporary fixes, don't satisfy. At the Well, we realize that we go from experience to experience, filling our lives with endless activities, hoping that the next thing will be the one that brings us joy; the next relationship, the next job, the next event . . . we even try to reinvent and recreate ourselves over and over, hoping that our "new ways" will bring about joy, pleasure, satisfaction, and fulfillment—*but they don't.* With each well we dig and with each time we draw "water," we realize that nothing satisfies . . . *in the long run.* Deep down, we know we'll be back. We fail to re-

empty.

alize our true need—for God Himself.

It's once we dig deeper, understanding that we desperately need God in greater ways than just for what He gives, we grasp that it is when we truly know God . . . *we begin to live.* Jesus was trying to get this woman to think more deeply about her life *and He succeeded.* The question is, did His words penetrate *our* souls . . . did *we* hear Him? He wants us to understand that we don't need all the things we're drawing from our own wells, we don't need all these things in life . . . we need a NEW LIFE!—a life in which we never thirst. In our emptiness, we realize that it is in truly knowing God, personally, as the only Source to provide our deepest needs where we will begin to truly live and be *filled to the full.*

The woman replies with excitement and anticipation, and in our emptiness we echo her exact words as we beg and plead with hope:

"Please, sir," the woman said,
"give me this water!
Then I'll never be thirsty again,
and I won't have to come here to get water."
John 4:15 (NIV)

As the woman reflects upon Jesus' words and we examine our own lives, Jesus replies in a way

empty.

that confuses the woman in greater ways than the absurd talk of "living water" . . . and Jesus' words crack open her cistern:

> *"Go and get your husband,"* Jesus told her.
> John 4:16 (NIV)

Seems like a simple request, *on the surface.* Quite possibly, Jesus just doesn't want her husband to miss out on this "living water" that He's about to give her. As an outsider looking in, this doesn't seem like *that odd* of a request. But, Jesus' gaze into her soul confronts what she would rather have hidden away.

Though this story takes a sudden turn into darkness, we're about to see God's grace poured out at this well *and* into this woman's life. His grace pours into yours too, once your soul is *poured out* and you allow Him to *dig deep* into your life.

empty.

Poured Out

Our journey to the well has taken an unexpected and confusing turn. Jesus decides to show this woman that the well in her life goes far deeper than she ever imagined. *And so does our own.* We learn that we can never *dwell* deeply unless we first *dig* deep; and until we're, first, completely *poured out.*

When the St. Louis bridge was being dug across the Mississippi River, the engineer who drew the plan said to the contractors, "You must go down till you strike the rock." The contractors said to the foreman, "You must go down till you strike the rock." And the foreman said to the men, "You must dig down deep till you strike the rock." And then they began digging. Day after day they dug, until one day the man said, "We have the rock!" They sent a piece of the rock up to the engineers who took a look at it and said, "No, that is

empty.

only sandstone; go down till you get the rock." So, they dug a few days more and said, "Now we have the rock," and again they sent up a piece; but the engineers said, "No, that is not rock yet; that is only a little harder sandstone." And they went on digging down deeper. But one day, they heard a great shout coming up from the men. This time they did not send up a piece to be examined. They said, "We have the rock." The engineers shouted back, "How do you know?" Back came more shouting, "We struck fire!"

Here's the thing, you'll know that you've struck the Rock . . . when you get fire. It is fire that God's presence comes out of (Leviticus 9:24), and it is through fire that He consumes (Deuteronomy 4:24). Don't ever stop digging, until you strike Fire—until you're one on one with the God Who is your Rock. When you've dug into the well of your soul, so deeply that you strike Fire, then you will know you're at the Source, and soon, you'll be drawing Living Water.

It's in getting one on one with God where HE is able to go deep into our souls and reveal to us our one and only true need that will fill up our emptiness. It's in our place of emptiness where we can come to understand that the deepest longings in our soul will never be satisfied till heaven. We

empty.

can't be afraid of the emptiness and all the emotions that come with it.

We must let the pain of disappointed longings drive us to The Well. We must allow our emptiness to open up a thirst we've never known before. In the emptiness of our lives, we find that beneath the surface, there is a longing that cannot be ignored, disguised, or submerged . . . no matter how desperately we might try to drown it out. The emptiness that consumes us is not to be filled by a gospel that preaches health and wealth. All too often, our faith tragically fails to flourish because instead of learning to be content *regardless* of our circumstances, we endlessly strive to rearrange and manipulate the details in our lives, in order to bring about a "temporary joy"—one that never lasts and never fully satisfies. We're not satisfied with *contented dissatisfaction*.

Digging

The woman at the well walked right into God's plan, we must never forget that *He* directs every detail of our lives (Psalm 27:3). Jesus suddenly began digging and the woman was oblivious to the well Jesus was about to dig into her soul:

empty.

"You are right when you say you have no husband.
The fact is, you have had five husbands,
and the man you now have is not your husband.
What you have just said is quite true."
John 4:17-18 (NIV)

We can imagine the intense silence. We can only begin to conceptualize that if Jesus revealed our darkest, deepest secret . . . how we might feel. Shock and disbelief doesn't even begin to describe the emotions, and awkward doesn't come close to adequately construing the circumstances.

But, the woman's situation is no different than our own, when it comes to Jesus confronting the areas of our lives that need addressing. And in the midst of her dire circumstances, she skirts the issue—changes the subject—in a desperate attempt to divert His attention. *Don't we do the same?*

"Sir," the woman said,
"I can see that you are a prophet.
Our ancestors worshiped on this mountain,
but you Jews claim that the place where we
must worship is in Jerusalem."
John 4:19-20 (NIV)

Talk about an abrupt change of subject! The woman suddenly opens the topic of "political, religious

empty.

matters," in an attempt to take the attention away from her sin. Jesus quickly responds, by basically telling her she's concerned with trivial things in life—things that simply don't matter. He tells her that it's not about *where* you worship, but *who* you worship. It's not about *religion*, it's about *relationship*. And this is good news for those who are disillusioned and discouraged after years of trying desperately to do everything right. We don't need more of *anything*—we need to let go of *everything*.

"Woman," Jesus replied, "believe me, a time is coming when you will worship the Father neither on this mountain nor in Jerusalem. You Samaritans worship what you do not know; we worship what we do know, for salvation is from the Jews. Yet a time is coming and has now come when the true worshipers will worship the Father in the Spirit and in truth, for they are the kind of worshipers the Father seeks. God is spirit, and his worshipers must worship in the Spirit and in truth."
John 4:21-24 (NIV)

If you're thirsty, Jesus' news is good: trying harder isn't the answer. Doing more isn't the solution. *You don't need to dig another well.* The truth that Jesus reveals to this woman, and the Good News that He has revealed to the world, shows

empty.

that our lives need to be confronted with the fact that it's the *internal* matters of our lives that need to be directly addressed. We're in desperate need of an extended exploration of our heart.

And this is where the digging begins—in this woman's life and *in our own.* The truth is, we thirst for what was lost at the Fall of man. We're intent on living our lives apart from God. We use strategies that are foolish, ineffective, and immoral, in the hopes of somehow quenching our thirst. Yet, nothing satisfies. We're faced with desires that we can't discard and pain that doesn't pass.

The truth is: *we're selfish.* We want life a certain way. We want people to treat us well. We want a good job and favorable financial status. We strive for pleasure and security. We want to love and be loved. We don't want flat tires and we don't want to have to wait in grocery store lines. And we're motivated by desires that we'd rather not discuss. It wouldn't be "Christian." It would reveal too much to really take a look inside ourselves. *So, we attempt to pray it away.* We beg God for the ability to overcome our desires, to no avail. And then we declare that God has failed us; or worse yet, that those desires are things that God has placed within us and that's why they won't go away.

But, when we come to the Well, when we come

empty.

to Jesus, we realize that it is not only "okay" to have the desires of our heart, but that it's okay to hurt. Jesus, before us, helps us to see that we must recognize that there is an unquenched thirst that must surface in our lives. And here's the harsh reality in the digging: sin is a much bigger problem than we think.

Our lives may be radically different from this woman's, on the surface, but the details are no matter . . . we, just like this woman, have an emptiness at the core of our soul that we don't want to face. The emptiness could come from a father that was never there, or worse, maybe, abusive. It may be due to an overprotective, smothering mother that left you feeling helpless or one who never loved you as a mother should. Quite possibly the emptiness comes from feeling inadequate as a husband or wife, which creates a desperate need to be appreciated and wanted. Maybe the emptiness comes from a friendship that ended up not being one at all, or from having a co-worker gossip behind your back until you ended up fired. Maybe it's an emptiness from knowing that your children don't have a relationship with Christ and the reality of that has emptied you to the point that you're not even sure God is actively seeking His lost sheep as He promises (Luke 15:4). The

empty.

emptiness can cast your faith into a deep, dark place; so much so, you're not sure you'll ever find it again.

We all have a story. *Our emptiness could write its own book.* But in the depths of our pain, we find an underlying truth: It's only when we face the horrific reality of our thirst for which no one and nothing can ever satisfy, will we turn to God in humble, broken dependence. To deny our thirst, or worse, to try to dig our own wells, is tragic at best. When we fail to face our deepest disappointments and admit our sinfulness, the best we can hope for is temporary, superficial change. God speaks clearly to us about the result of trying to fill our own emptiness:

"They dress the wound of my people as though it were not serious. 'Peace, peace,' they say, when there is no peace." (Jeremiah 6:14 NIV)

God doesn't want us hiding from Him. We should have learned that in the Garden of Eden. We should have learned that we CAN'T hide anything from Him:

"Nothing in all creation is hidden from God's sight. Everything is uncovered and laid bare before the eyes of him to whom we must give account."
Hebrews 4:13 (NIV)

empty.

The woman at the well couldn't hide anything from God and neither can we. Relieving our pain is not the goal—emptying ourselves to be filled is. We need to be poured out. And that is painful. It's because our heart is deceitful that we don't typically recognize the core sin in our heart—which we need to deal with through repentance (Jeremiah 17:9). The emptying, the pouring out, though painful, has a powerful purpose. The emptying is necessary; because it is only through a deep awareness of our pain, due to profound disappointments in our lives, where we realize our deepest desire that has been masked by our endless attempts to seek relief from our present suffering. And our well digging comes from the sin in our heart. And here's the sad truth: VERY few people are willing to deeply embrace the pain and disappointment they have experienced in life. The person that has heard what Jesus has said at the well realizes that pain is not the problem—"It's my desperate attempts to relieve the pain that is the core sin of my heart. It's my unwillingness to pour out my life for Jesus, so that He can fill me, which is causing my emptiness."

Our emptiness will do one of two things: harden our hearts, or drive us deeper in trusting God. Thankfully, the woman at the well saw the little

empty.

faith she had spring into a well that filled her to the full. But, first, she had to face the pain of her past. Sin stood in the way of getting the Water she needed to quench her thirst. We, just like this woman find ourselves wasting effort and energy digging our own wells—and worse, digging broken ones.

We fail, miserably, to grasp the fact that only God can supply what our soul most deeply desires. When our heart's longings are not satisfied, there is a deep, unexplainable pain that must be addressed. And "time" does not heal or help all things. The only thing time does is allow us the ability to go into denial or temporarily escape the circumstances. In times of emptiness, we can do ourselves more harm than good by seeking momentary pleasures—reaching out for encouragement in all kinds of neurotic ways. We end up drawing a bucket of sand, instead of water. We find ourselves living with the consequences of living unsatisfied lives. In our emptiness, we see life as an indescribable cruel experience that resembles what hell must be like. So, when we hear mention of Living Water, *it gets our attention*. But, first, we need to take an inside look at why we thirst. We're going to need to dig deep.

What we know is that the "Christian Life" con-

empty.

tinually causes people to turn from it, rather than to it. And it's in looking at our emptiness that we find our reluctance to examine our thirst, our discouragement and despair, because it appears to violate what most call a "victorious" life. Get this straight: Jesus NEVER asked us to deny our pain and cover it with Christianity. Far too many "Christians" are living less than victorious lives for one reason: dealing with what's really going on inside is too uncomfortable, disturbing, and embarrassing. They find themselves "coping" with life, instead of "overcoming" it. And they'd rather just hide it . . . from others and themselves. But that's the purpose of digging. It loosens up what's been trenched inside, and the *excavation* leads to *renovation*.

Without the digging, we find ourselves moving steadily along life's path, without ever stopping to address the deep pain in our soul. If we'll see the digging as a way to Living Water, if we'll understand it to be the beginning to a more intimate relationship with the Living God, then isn't it worth any temporary pain that might surface in the process? We have a choice to make: stay buried in the dirt, or allow God to dig us out of our hole so that we might truly live (Psalm 40:2).

Our emptiness, our thirst, is to make us fully

empty.

aware of our unsatisfied soul. And if you don't know Jesus, if you're not meeting with Him one on one, you won't be able to have your thirst quenched by Living Water and your emptiness will relentlessly drive you to temporary relief from your pain. Our pain and suffering in life demands relief; in some way, our souls *must* find relief.

If we'll face our pain, embrace the emptiness, and allow it to drive us to the only One who can quench our thirst . . . we will truly never thirst again. Yet, don't misunderstand this. We might be "thirsty," but we'll never "thirst." Being "thirsty" is temporary. The word "thirst" insinuates an on-going condition in this context. We will need to go to the Well, *continually*. And it's because life is difficult, at best. Our happiness is typically rooted in the hope of our present circumstances, instead of simple hope in God. And life is fallen. A minor ache in our heart can explode into excruciating pain when we hear insults from friends, harsh words from a spouse, encounter financial destruction, agonize from a disrespectful a child, and endure the endless tragedies of life that seems to offer no mercy. Daily, we will face profound disappointments . . . and we will be *thirsty*.

Yet, if we weren't thirsty, we wouldn't need to drink. And without that thirst to bring us to the

empty.

Well, we'd never experience one on one time with Jesus. We'd miss out on Living Water. We're thirsty because we need more of Jesus. Although we're not aware of it, although our belief is that we simply need a drink of water in a dry and weary land, He knows what we really need, and it's what satisfies. We're oblivious that our heart has deceived us and He needs to open our heart *and* our eyes. We need to be able to see life through His eyes, not our own—and we'll need to examine our heart, as He reveals His. Our response to a God whose love for us knows no bounds should be none less than the words in John and Charles Wesley's hymn from *Hymn's on the Lord's Supper*:

Take my soul and body's powers,
Take my memory, mind and will;
All my goods and all my hours,
All I know or think or feel,
All I speak and all I do,
Take my heart, but make it new.
How blest are they who still abide,
Close sheltered in Thy bleeding side;
Who thence their strength and life derive,
And by Thee move, and in Thee live.

We're told to love the Lord with all our heart, soul, strength, and mind, *and we know we don't.*

empty.

Life has a way of causing us to easily toss aside such commandments. We fail to see our daily battle as an *eternal* one. And we miss the point. We're worried about small stuff, and we overlook the heart of the matter. And Jesus tells us we've got it wrong (Mark 7:6-8, 20-23):

6 *He replied, "Isaiah was right when he prophesied about you hypocrites; as it is written:*

"'These people honor me with their lips,
   but their hearts are far from me.
7 *They worship me in vain;*
   their teachings are merely human rules.'

8 *You have let go of the commands of God and are holding on to human traditions."*

20 *He went on: "What comes out of a person is what defiles them.* 21 **For it is from within, out of a person's heart, that evil thoughts come** *— sexual immorality, theft, murder,* 22 *adultery, greed, malice, deceit, lewdness, envy, slander, arrogance and folly.* 23 *All these evils come from inside and defile a person."*

Our emptiness brings us to a place where we're aware something is desperately wrong inside. Though we reluctantly admit it, because we're not sure we'll make it through the process, we know that we need God to reorganize, reno-

empty.

vate, and restore our heart—we need to be *poured out.*

The Heart of the Matter

Jesus speaks of Living Water in a way that captures our soul and thrusts our heart wide open. And that's exactly what He wants. We, just like the woman at the well, need God to dig deep into our heart because that's where the dirt is keeping the wellspring of Living Water from coming forth. And we haven't been guarding it (our heart) like we should. The dirt has been piling up over the years and we're too weary to dig it out.

> *"Above all else, guard your heart,*
> *for everything you do flows from it."*
> Proverbs 4:23 (NIV)

We see our world and interpret reality as a result of what we've become through life experiences. Our life, and how we view it all, is a result of what is in the depths of our being. It's from that perspective that we make choices, take action, and make desperate attempts to change our reality. We live from within the depths of our soul—most of

empty.

which we barely understand. Our greatest need is not water, but a *renewed* heart. The way we've been looking at our life's circumstances has been tainted by our humanity and we've been making choices and taking actions that have habitually been done apart from God. It's our heart that needs to be transformed so that we might have a *relevant* and *real* relationship with Jesus.

And there's a lot of work to do. Living Water changes us from the inside out; it changes our ideas, beliefs, feelings, habits, choices, and multiple other facets of our character. The digging, God does, penetrates through the deepest layers of our soul until He reaches the core—until He strikes the Rock in your soul.

We can find ourselves attempting to find another way, other than the painful process of digging that God has begun—at times we even shove God aside and declare we'd rather just do the job ourselves. We spend endless effort, extraordinary strength, and wasted time trying to dig a well that may lead to "something," but not Living Water. It's Living Water we need when we need answers to the deepest longings of humanity. We need answers on righteousness, provision, and purpose. Our wells will never answer those questions; in fact, they only create more confusion in our efforts

empty.

to answer what only God can.

Without Jesus, without Living Water, we will ponder, endlessly, questions like: "Why are we here? What keeps the world going? Is this a world of chaos or order?" Without answers to these questions, life will flood our soul and drown it out at the mercy of whatever life circumstances we're subjected to. It's what's within that makes all the difference—it's the heart. And no matter how hard we try, *we can't change what only God can.* And we can't hide what God can clearly see.

"The LORD *doesn't see things the way you see them. People judge by outward appearance, but the* LORD *looks at the heart."* (1 Samuel 16:7 NLT)

The life that we live, the choices we make, and the emotions that are exhibited in our hours, days, and years, well up from a depth of hidden motives that are just too risky to reveal. Seldom do we realize the deepest level of our souls. We're too busy, too tired and discouraged, or too afraid to dig that deep.

And what we find is that as the dirt piles up in our hearts, things start growing in it. Things we never planted. And they take on a life of their own. They grow and grow, until one day we real-

empty.

ize we're in need of desperate help. Our only hope is in the God Who does the *impossible*. Only He can fully release us from being at the mercy of our hurting heart, through the love of His own. Only God can save us; and the emptiness brings us to a place of crying out in desperation:

"Search me, O God, and know my heart; test me and know my anxious thoughts. Point out anything in me that offends you, and lead me along the path of everlasting life." (Psalm 138:23-24 NLT)

As God searches, and clearly knows, our heart, He starts to point, just like He did at the woman at the well . . . and our defenses go up. We know that what He's pointing at is too difficult to discuss—too complex to go into. We'd rather just ignore it . . . maybe then it'll simply go away. But it doesn't . . . and emptiness remains.

All of our efforts will be in vain if we're striving, through our own efforts to become like Jesus. Living to conform and *act* in a way that is righteous or worthy is attempting the *impossible*. In our declared devotion to Christ, through religious means, we, like the woman at the well, "know" plenty about Jesus, but we really don't *know* Him. If we did, we'd know our true condition and we'd

empty.

allow Him to dig.

In our emptiness, we find ourselves facing an inescapable human problem with no earthly solution. *We're thirsty and nothing satisfies.* Our heart is broken and nothing fixes it. But, when Jesus steps into the picture, He talks about Living Water, and with little effort, He turns us inside out . . . and He captures our attention in ways that nothing has. We realize, that at this moment, at the well, nothing else, but Jesus, matters. And His Words strike deep and they dig to depths we didn't know, until our pain meets God's grace and something miraculous happens.

Revelation takes the place of confusion, and Jesus breaks our hearts and binds it up all at once (Psalm 147:3). Through the digging process, we can clearly see the pile of dirt. Our heart isn't a servant's one, but one of idolatry. And we've got it all wrong. We've confused God's intended order of things; we've put together a priority list of our own, and instead of a life that is ordered like this:

God
Spirit
Mind (Thoughts and Emotions)
Soul
Body

empty.

we're living life in exactly the reverse order. And God suddenly drops to the bottom of the list. We've had our mind set on the flesh, and we've forgotten how that ends:

> *"The mind governed by the flesh is death,*
> *but the mind governed by the*
> *Spirit is life and peace."*
> Romans 8:6 (NIV)

Death. Isn't that what emptiness feels like? And *the heart of the matter is that our heart hasn't mattered much*, except that we've allowed our flesh to dictate it and drive it into despair. It's that second part of Romans 8:6 we're after—the life and peace part. We need Living Water. And we go back to the well . . .

At the well, we're all taken back at how insensitive Jesus seems to be by bringing up this woman's sin so directly. It's seems brutal at best. And it's clear that her life is not working out so "well." She's obviously struggling and unhappy, so why would He make matters worse? Why would a loving God do this? Why does He allow us to experience further pain *when we're already in the depths of it*? It's simple: God *wants* us to feel the pain. *Pain is our pathway to God*. When the world doesn't satis-

empty.

fy, *He wants us to clearly understand that He alone does.* To deny our pain is to cast aside what Christ did on the Cross. The Cross reveals that there is good beneath the bad—there is joy behind the pain—there is fullness after emptiness—there is Living Water in the dry desert of our lives.

We all face disappointments; therefore, we hurt. But, as we'll learn through this woman's life, at the well . . . when we make relieving our pain the priority of our life, we take a tragic detour in our faith and we abandon our pursuit of God. *Our thirst has purpose.* Our *emptiness,* our pain, our thirst, causes us to not hold too tightly to the things of this world. This is not our home and God never wants us to forget that. And we can't be deceived—sometimes God's path takes us into deeper pain and disappointment in this world. The woman at the well just wanted a simple drink of water, but Jesus offered her something more . . . something that emptied her soul in greater ways than she ever thought possible.

The digging does something powerful—it accomplishes much more than we ever anticipated. Through the painful process, we become aware of our greater spiritual need, without us even realizing it. The deeper we go, the more eager we are to desperately seek God. We become aware of our

empty.

current condition—with a growing realization of what is really occurring in our lives and in our relationships . . . with a greater desire to stop pretending it's something that it's not. Through each shovel of dirt, we find an internal stillness, a loss of energy that develops from realizing that nothing we can do, in our own strength and resources, can ever satisfy our deepest longings. And in those paralyzing, yet riveting moments, we anticipate hitting the wellspring. Deep down we know God is digging for a reason. He finds purpose in everything—at least we've been believing that in faith. It seems that in order to get to the Source, it's imperative to go far below the surface, where things are dark, hidden, and concealed.

This woman was no different than we are—she encountered the hard truth . . . that being confronted over sin, being poured out, hurts, *deeply*. The moment at the well helps us to see that God can meet us in our struggles, in our attempt to bury what must be dug up. He is there, in our emptiness. He never leaves our side and never abandons us to our sin and shame. Throughout the process we can be certain that it is God Himself Who is doing the digging. His presence is assured in the process and He's there to complete what He's begun.

empty.

"And I am certain that God, who began the good work within you, will continue his work until it is finally finished on the day when Christ Jesus returns."
Philippians 1:6 (NLT)

And as He meets us, as we're poured out, and He begins to dig, something happens. Something we never anticipated and *neither did the woman at the well.*

Living Water

We get defensive when we're confronted with the wrongs in our lives. The woman at the well was no different. She basically responded in the way we do, at times, to God: *"I don't need your help."*

*The woman said, "I know that Messiah
(called Christ) is coming.
When he comes, he will explain everything to us."*
John 4:25 (NIV)

In layman's terms, she said, "Butt out." And we do the same. When God starts digging in our lives, we'd rather He just mind His own business. (Doesn't He have enough going on to keep Him

empty.

busy?) In fact, we often go back to digging our own wells. (Sometimes different ones—or just simply digging deeper in the ones we've already dug.) We can even become aggravated that He interrupted our work!

In a moment that changed her life forever, the woman heard words that instantly filled her to the full:

> *Then Jesus declared,*
> *"I, the one speaking to you—I am he."*
> John 4:26 (NIV)

In an instant, the woman's soul was poured out *and* was suddenly filled. And we see the Living Water that Jesus promised this woman begin to flow.

> *"Then, leaving her water jar,*
> *the woman went back to the town and said*
> *to the people, 'Come, see a man who told me*
> *everything I ever did. Could this be the Messiah?'*
> *They came out of the town*
> *and made their way toward him."*
> John 4:28-30 (NIV)

Something happened. Did you miss it? *She left her jar.* A realization took hold of her soul . . . *she*

empty.

wasn't thirsty anymore. So, what was it about this Living Water that filled her so much? We desperately need what she experienced. We need a better understanding of this Living Water and how it is that it satisfies.

We first have to take a look at what this Living Water is and what it's not. The truth is that Jesus, when promising Living Water, did not promise to give us comfort, pleasure, financial success, and never-ending bliss. The question arises, as Jesus talks about this Living Water, that if he's not promising to drown out the pain, He's promising something entirely different with this Water. In fact, it appears that He's promising *peace* **in the depths** of our *pain*. But, it seems hardly possible to live in peace and rest amid the tragic circumstances of our lives. And the Promise drives us to the Well.

When we're thirsty, Jesus says we're to go the Well, we're to go to Him:

"Let anyone who is thirsty come to me and drink.
Whoever believes in me,
as Scripture has said, rivers of living water
will flow from within them."
John 7:37-39 (NIV)

---

empty.

The Living Water flows from *within*. And if it flows from within, then it's there where He must dig a well. Our soul is the declared excavation site. It's where there is exposure, processing, and recording. (Precisely what happened at the well.)

To understand the significance of wells, we can go back and look at biblical days, when groundwater was accessed through the digging of wells. *That's how life was sustained.* We find in Genesis 26 that Isaac, along with his family, servants and flocks, were forced to change their location and move because of their need for water. Isaac reopened wells that his father Abraham had used. In Genesis 26:25, we find that when Isaac moved to the new place, he built and altar, pitched his tent, and dug a well. When Isaac's servants located water, he found a permanent dwelling place for his family and flocks. *We need a Source.* A place where we can dwell and be certain we will be filled, in order to sustain our lives.

When God goes to digging wells, in order to fill us with Living Water, He has a process. And it's always the same, though the details (dirt) may vary.

First and foremost, *God chooses the ground where He begins to dig.* (One thing we need to learn very quickly: we must come to God on His terms, not

empty.

our own.) The area of our lives in which He chooses to dig is no concern of ours. He knows what He's doing. Jesus' Divine appointment that day with the woman at the well was not one she had made, but One God Himself had orchestrated. And know this, whatever your greatest disappointment is in life, that's where God will do the digging. He's about to shovel out the dirt that is clogging your life and keeping Him out. He wants to rearrange your priorities and transform your heart. He's making all things *new*, not better.

"For I am about to do something new. See, I have already begun! Do you not see it? I will make a pathway through the wilderness. I will create rivers in the dry wasteland." (Isaiah 43:19 NLT)

And in order to make all things new, He will ask us to take an inward look at our lives in the areas of home and family, church and ministry, community, relationships, jobs, or attitudes—the list could go on. It's where there are disappointments, dreams gone bad, and desires that prioritize your daily life where the digging will begin.

Just as the woman at the well, God will open our hearts, and then the work will begin. And it's a painful process because it opens up the *pain* in-

empty.

side. It shows us the core of who we are and it's not a pretty sight. Though we'd rather cast the uglier parts of our lives in the depths of darkness, Jesus brings them into the Light—so they can be dealt with—eliminated, poured out, so our souls can be filled.

We need a Savior . . . each and every moment of our life, not just for one day at Calvary. When we realize our need for Him, in greater ways than just the satisfaction of our salvation, then we can prepare for the work He's about to do in our lives and brace ourselves for a miracle.

"Hardship often prepares an ordinary person for an extraordinary destiny." —C.S. Lewis

Secondly, *God will bring us to a place of resolve—realizing our condition and our desperate need for Him.* He allows us to thirst so that He can provide the Living Water. We're empty so that He can fill us to the full. This place of resolve is a realization that we want God to move in our lives. It's a time when we're ready for the digging to begin. It's when we see that our emptiness has purpose and that God has a plan—and we surrender—everything. It's in this place of resolve that we, just like the woman at the well, declare, *". . . give me this water . . ."* (John 4:15 NIV).

empty.

Third, *God will break the ground of our soul and begin to dig*—just as He did with the woman in the well. He reveals something in our lives that's just not right. (But note: this can never happen without "one on one" time with Jesus.) And He'll begin to reveal the places in your heart that just aren't in line with His will. In this phase, it's about turning to His Word, what He says, and beginning to grasp that what Jesus says and what is Promised within the Bible is Truth. The woman at the well found herself turned inside out when Jesus told her "everything she ever did" (John 4:28). He knows everything you've done as well. All of that is no matter to Him, He's drawing you near so that you can draw water from Him—Living Water. He knows that you're drowning in your desires and He knows your thirst. That's why He's at the well. He knows it's where you'll come to Him— thirsty—ready to drink, deeply.

Fourth, *dry ground is hard to dig in*. Have you ever pulled weeds? Which is better, dry dirt or damp? Dry dirt holds the roots tight and it's the trials of your life and your greatest disappointments that have created the dry ground that hold the roots to your hardened heart. You'd think that all the tears you've cried would have softened the dirt to the point of being mud, but instead, those

empty.

tears have dried up your heart and that's why you're empty. The water within has gone dry, and your heart has lost all hope . . . in your emptiness, you don't even have the temporary joy of seeing a mirage.

Know this: God is fully and properly prepared for the excavation that needs to occur in your soul. He's up for the job. God's strength is greater than man's weakness:

"God's weakness is stronger than the greatest of human strength." (1 Corinthians 1:25 NLT)

God is able to do MORE than we can hope for or imagine:

"Now to him who is able to do immeasurably more than all we ask or imagine, according to his power that is at work within us." (Ephesians 3:20 NIV)

The hard dry ground of your soul is no challenge for God. But, you'll need to allow Him to do the digging. You'll be tempted to walk away. The woman at the well could have become offended by Jesus prying into her life, but instead, with her heart wide open, she recognized Him for who He was . . . her Savior. The one on one time with Jesus

empty.

can be difficult, but the well He's digging in your soul is worth the pain of the shoveling.

Fifth, *it's about the Water, not the dirt.* Too often, through this digging process, we become weary of waiting for God to get the job done. We argue that He's done quite enough digging. We start looking at the pile of dirt, the things that have gone so wrong in our spirit, mind, body, and soul . . . and we're tempted to see it as a never-ending process. Here's the thing: Keep your eyes on Jesus. Keep focused on the Water. There will be plenty of dirt to get through before you strike Living Water, but NOTHING is too difficult for God (Jeremiah 32:17). Trust Him to not only do the job, but to be your provision through it.

We desperately need Living Water. Our thirst cannot be quenched without it. When we see that Living Water is used throughout Scripture to represent giving and promoting life in limitless supply, we, just like the woman at the well, are desperate for God to give it to us. Though it's a process, we can be sure of the result. We're assured that rivers of Living Water will flow from within us:

*"Anyone who believes in me may come and drink! For the Scriptures declare, **'Rivers of living water will flow from his heart.'"** (John 7:38 NLT)*

empty.

As God does the well digging, so that this Living Water can spring forth, you must understand that the most important part of this process is realizing that *you're with Jesus.* The woman at the well could hardly contain herself when she realized she was speaking to the Messiah that was promised to come. At the moment Jesus struck the rock within her heart, He hit Water. And her spirit began to overflow with a wellspring that caused her to leave behind her water jar and burst into the city to share that she had met Jesus (John 4:39-42 NIV):

Many of the Samaritans from that town believed in him because of the woman's testimony, "He told me everything I ever did." So when the Samaritans came to him, they urged him to stay with them, and he stayed two days. And because of his words many more became believers.

They said to the woman, "We no longer believe just because of what you said; now we have heard for ourselves, and we know that this man really is the Savior of the world."

The people of the city knew the woman *well* (pun intended). They were quite aware of her life and had witnessed her life to that point. But even *they* saw something that changed *their* hearts. They saw water coming from a rock. Don't quite get that? Let's understand it better . . .

empty.

Water from the Rock

We need to take a deep look at this situation and our lives. If we want to understand this thoroughly, we'll find ourselves in Exodus 17. Keep in mind: this is after God's chosen people had been freed of slavery. This is *after* the parting of the Red Sea. There was complaining, grumbling, and desperation. There was a demand that God show up. And there was doubt that He *could* or that He *would*.

"'I will stand before you on the rock at Mount Sinai. Strike the rock, and water will come gushing out. Then the people will be able to drink.' So Moses struck the rock as he was told, and water gushed out as the elders looked on." (Exodus 17:6 NIV)

So here's the thing: This wasn't the first time the Children of Israel were complaining—they complained at the bitter waters of Marah that they had nothing to drink. But that was early on, this is at Rephidim. God had delivered them from tragedy several times, provided them fresh manna daily, and continually poured down His grace to sustain them. These weren't desperate people in survival mode; they had witnessed God's grace in action, first hand. These are complaints that are lodged by people exaggerating their desperation

empty.

and clamoring for ease and comfort. They're disappointed by their hardship and struggling with discontent over the possibility that they might be denied, even for one moment, life's necessities.

The truth is that the Children of Israel knew, full well, that God would not let them die in the wilderness—He'd preserved them far too many times. He'd worked miracle upon miracle to bring them to the very place where they shouted at Him. But, the people weren't willing to wait on God. And most of the time, *neither are we*. We want to be satisfied NOW. We, just like the Israelites, seek to interject OUR will into God's plan. Our prayers take a drastic turn from *requests* to *demands*. And that changes the whole scene.

The complaining at Rephidim was under different circumstances, and the method of deliverance needed to be more impactful. At Marah, God took bitter waters and made them sweet. Seems the Israelites were not all that impressed. So, this time, God decides to bring life-giving waters from a *rock*. How exactly does one take a solid stone in a dry and barren land and cause it to bring forth a river from which a multitude of people can drink? We suddenly hear words echoing throughout history and into our empty hearts,

"Is anything too hard for the Lord?"
Genesis 18:14 (NLT)

empty.

In a moment of doubt, amidst the miracles, God brings water from the rock—*their thirst was satisfied.*

> *"He opened the rock,*
> *and water gushed out;*
> *like a river it flowed in the desert."*
> Psalm 105:41 (NLT)

We take a look at Living Water and we see that God uses it to represent something that is vital to *our* survival. We are to drink from the Rock. And the Rock is Christ:

> *". . . and all of them drank the same spiritual water.*
> *For they drank from the spiritual rock that*
> *traveled with them, and that rock was Christ."*
> 1 Corinthians 10:4 (NLT)

Here we are told that the Rock in Horeb is Christ. Jesus, our Rock is from which Living Waters flow. We see the prophecy of our thirst being quenched from Isaiah 55:1:

> *"Come, all you who are thirsty,*
> *come to the waters;"*

All we have to do is come—just as the woman at the well did. In her thirst, she met Jesus, and that changed EVERYTHING.

We have taken a deeper look into this moment at the well and found principles to apply to our

empty.

own lives, but we may have missed something. We might have overlooked the thing that changed this woman. What was it that altered the course of the conversation AND her life? Did you notice it? *It was what Jesus said.* His Words struck the rock, in her heart, and Living Water burst forth. So here's the thing: If we want Living Water, if we are desperate to be filled in our emptiness, we need to know what Jesus is saying to us. *Do you know what He's saying to you?* He's brought you to the well, with a thirst that only faith in Him can satisfy. We find ourselves empty, thirsty, because we're continually pursuing hope that quenches in the "here and now"; it's a hope that *never* satisfies—our hope in Christ can never be for this life alone. If we are filled only by our circumstantial happiness, then all *true* hope really IS gone and *we will thirst.*

"And if our hope in Christ is only for this life,
we are more to be pitied than anyone in the world."
1 Corinthians 15:19 (NLT)

And here is where Living Water *quenches.* Our emptiness keeps us longing, not for what is in this world, but for what lies in eternity. It is the hope of what is in heaven that will sustain us, shift our discouragement, and demand a patient surrender that leaves us satisfied. Living Water provides us

empty.

the fountain that enables us to serve God and live out our purposes in any circumstance, keeping our vision anchored on the Cross. It's our faith that is sustained by our Hope in Christ and what He's done on our behalf that satisfies the soul. And here's what Living Water looks like in *your* life:

—Giving *love* to a lost spouse, a prodigal child, or a hurtful friend
—Bringing *joy* to the most hurting heart
—Living in *peace* while your financial world crumbles
—Showing *patience* when time is running out
—Being *kind* when you'd rather not
—Doing *good* things for others when everything in your life has gone bad
—Walking in *faith* when you can't see the very next step in front of you
—*Gently* responding to those who cause discord in your life
—Exhibiting *self-control* when life is spiraling *out* of control

It's the Living Water that nourishes the fruit of the Spirit (Galatians 5:22-23: love, joy, peace, patience, kindness, goodness, faithfulness, gentleness, and self-control).

empty.

Living Water enables us to be filled to the full with the Truth that God is doing good at every moment, in every circumstance—that even in our troubles and through our trials, He is blessing us with His presence and His power.

We, just like the woman at the well, don't realize that what we're really yearning for is an encounter with God. We dig our own wells in an effort to satisfy our thirst and ignore the Living Water that God is continually offering.

It's when you're thirsty, at the well, you'll learn:

1. *God's desire is to bless you.* Although we might find plenty of circumstantial evidence to the contrary, God loves to bless us in extravagant ways. He's not withholding His best from you, He's promised just the opposite: *"the LORD bestows favor . . . no good thing does he withhold from those whose walk is blameless"* (Psalm 84:11). What if you were to see your situation as a blessing? What if there's a component of your life that you can't quite see and God is actually blessing you in a way that you can't understand. What if you dared to believe that He is God and you are not? What if you trusted God that your *pathway of pain* is *a journey to joy?*

empty.

2. *Your deepest desire is to have an encounter with God*. We tend to continually strive toward lesser pleasures in life, rather than the indescribable pleasure of God Himself. Amid the crises in life, we forsake our "first love": *"You don't love me or each other as you did at first* (Revelation 2:4 NLT)! It is only when we desire God alone that He gives us the desires of our heart: *"Delight yourself in the Lord and he will give you the desires of your heart"* (Psalm 37:4 NLT). First things first. We need to understand our true need. We must grasp the reason for our emptiness—it's so that we will desire God.

3. *The emptiness in life awakens your desire for God*. A prime example of how God uses ALL things for good is how He allows our emptiness to bring about a thirst that drives us to the Well. Our emptiness is not without purpose, it's an opportunity to unleash God's power. In a moment, not unlike the moment the woman at the well experienced, you will still experience your pain, but you will no longer demand relief from it—you'll find peace for your soul in knowing that God is with you. Because here's the hard core truth: Cancer will claim a loved ones' life, drunkenness will lead to cirrhosis, the divorce will happen, broken friendships will fail to be restored, the pregnancy

empty.

may not happen, lost income will cause a foreclosure, loneliness may continue for a life-time, *and
God will stand by and do nothing.* You will be miser-
able and you will feel all kinds of feelings towards
God that you're not "supposed" to feel. You'll be
empty and discouraged. You'll spend more time
worrying than worshipping and praying will seem
pointless. Your soul will print out a flat line and
you'll be unable to resuscitate it. And you'll realize that *nothing* but God can save you. When
you're thirsty, nothing but His Living Water will
satisfy—that's what He wants you to know. *That's
why you're empty.*

When your soul is thirsty, eliminating the
troubles of life is not what satisfies, it's whatever
comes from God—whoever He is . . . in your intolerable thirst, you find, at the Well, that when
you're poured out . . . *God is enough.* And He fills
you to the full—just as He did the woman at the
well.

Here's the thing: One woman changed the lives
of many because of a moment by a well. One moment in your relationship with Jesus can alter the
course of your life as well. It's about going to The
Well, drawing near to Him continually, and getting one on one. Let Him dig, as much as is needed. Know that the dirt outside the well of your

empty.

soul that's piling up is evidence that you're being emptied, poured out, and Jesus is about to spring up a fountain of Living Water within you. What you're thirsty for isn't what you think—you're not thirsty for "water," you're thirsty for Truth. You're being emptied, so that you'll live *full of faith*.

empty.

Chapter 4

Full of Faith

Jesus said in John 10:9-11 (NIV):

> *"I am the gate; whoever enters through me will be*
> *saved. He will come in and go out, and find pasture.*
> *The thief comes only to steal and kill and destroy;*
> ***I have come that they may have life,***
> ***and have it to the full."***

We endlessly try, in desperate attempts, to fill our emptiness through a physical world; yet the only thing that satisfies is found in a spiritual realm. All the world's resources will never satisfy our *true* thirst. And although we'd rather acquire Living Water another way, it seems inevitable that it is only found by digging into a deep hole of darkness that forms a well in our heart. The kind of faith and hope we want is not what we think. On the surface, we just want things in life to go

empty.

"well." We don't want to have problems in relationships, we'd prefer to have our bank accounts continually replenished with little to no effort, we'd like our children to honor us and show us utmost respect and love, we'd like our spouse to get on their knees each day in prayer for us and our family, we'd like to always have a clean bill of health and tears to never fall. But that's not the way life happens . . . *is it*? The truth is that relationships are damaged beyond repair, we face financial ruin, lost children end up on drugs and in jail, spouses betray us through more ways than we can count, our health fails, and tears fall continuously until we're certain we'll drown in them. We need our souls filled, *but not in the way we think*.

True hope does not come from a blissful life, but a life that is filled with doubt, yet walks in faith and peace—regardless of the circumstances. Without THAT hope, *there is no other*.

Our emptiness has purpose. It opens the way for God to begin to dig a well. And in the process, we learn to see what really matters, what's of value and what's not. Emptiness destroys false expectations and helps us to discover *true* hope. It's through this process, while God digs into our heart, that the Rock springs forth the Living Water which brings about something we never thought

empty.

possible in our lives—joy.

That hope, that peace, that joy, doesn't come from the *resolution* of our circumstances. It's not when God wraps life up and puts a pretty bow on it. It's when we realize that we can trust Him, *no matter what happens.* It is a beautiful, breath-taking resolve that doesn't demand, but simply desires ... God alone.

We can look to Jesus in His strength, but also in His weakness. As we're tempted to toss aside what little faith we have left and discount God's character, we find Jesus in a dark place in the Garden of Gethsemane. At arguably the most crucial moment in history, Jesus, King of Kings, seemed to collapse . . . and He did it in front of three of His closest friends. Here's what Jesus, our Lord and Savior, told them:

"My soul is overwhelmed to the point of death."
Matthew 26:38 (NIV)

And He asked for them to stay, watch, and pray. The Lord of Lords saw more power in *prayer* than any other resource available to Him.

With all the miracles Jesus had performed, with His evident power over all creation as God incarnate . . . how was it that His soul could reach

empty.

this point? Jesus was facing the temptation to quit. He knew we'd face our own. And His personal battle on the Mount of Olives, the place where He agonized and wept bitterly to the point of sweating blood, became the very place where He ascended into heaven a few weeks later.

Deep inside, we're compelled and drawn by Jesus' tenacity and commitment to such a horrific sacrifice. In a strange way, it stirs up a powerful strength within us to walk forward in simple hope in Him. But, when we're suddenly faced with the reality of our circumstances in life, we realize we'd rather life just go "well," *rather than become more like Jesus*. But throughout the Bible, we come to understand that there's no shortcut to joy. We find God confuses, frustrates, and disassembles our relationship with Him in order to deepen it. We can become discouraged to the point of self-hatred, and it is Jesus, whom we continually betray, who tells us, "Don't lose hope." He assures us in the Garden of Gethsemane that God has a plan that's unfolding that we can't clearly see. He wants us to know this in our own lives as well. He shows us that even when He *knew* God's plan, He still hurt, He still experienced anguish, He asked God to change the plan, He was crushed to the point of His soul collapsing . . . but *He didn't lose hope*. And

empty.

He tells us, through keeping His eyes focused on His purpose, that more than anything we desire, our deepest desire is to live for Him, to further the Kingdom of God, and to be in relationship with Him. He shows us how God alone satisfies the emptiness in our soul, *no matter what happens.*

The Facts of Faith

There always comes a moment in the digging, when the dirt is piling up in your life, where faith just doesn't seem to apply. You've trusted God and He appears to be completely untrustworthy. The divorce was finalized, the cancer spread, your addicted spouse ended up in rehab, your wayward child landed themselves in jail, the foreclosure happened, and you didn't get the job. Faith loses out when we realize that God could have done something . . . and *He did nothing.*

God frustrates our faith with His inconsistency and His ridiculous and draining unpredictability. Life *seems* completely random, when He's promised us it's not. *If He's involved in every detail of our lives, why is it that it seems He overlooks so many?* We're empty and it seems God is draining us even more. *And He is.* He's digging a well of Living Wa-

empty.

ter, the only way a well can be dug, from the inside out. And it's in the process that we learn a few things:

1. *We must abandon our desires for this life.* This isn't easily done. In fact, we'll need the God of impossibilities . . . because this lesson of faith is, by all indications of our soul, *impossible—without God.* If we're to fulfill God's purposes in our lives, we're going to have to relinquish our own. This is probably the most critical factor in our faith, when it comes to growing spiritually. But, we can't do it on our own. And that's why we have Jesus. And the Holy Spirit is our guide. This is where it all begins—surrender. Surrendering everything. Letting go of it all. And it's okay to weep bitterly over what will be lost. Jesus has never asked us to mask our pain. If *He* didn't, why would He expect *us* to? He only wants a genuine relationship with you, *nothing less.*

2. *We must acknowledge our pain.* Emptiness creates a pain all of its own. In fact, in the midst of our emptiness, we sometimes conclude that we won't survive it. And we're right. The emptiness pours out the old life, so that God can make it new. He's promised us He'll do that. So don't be

empty.

surprised when it feels like He's ripping out your heart, because He is:

> *"And I will give you a new heart,*
> *and I will put a new spirit in you.*
> *I will take out your stony,*
> *stubborn heart and give you a tender,*
> *responsive heart."*
> Ezekiel 36:26 (NLT)

Your pain is not the evidence of your weak faith, it's an indication that your human. Pain is part of the process. It was true at the Cross, and it's true in *your* life.

"It is doubtful that God can use a man greatly until he's been broken deeply."—C.S. Lewis

Discovering the things in life that are truly wonderful, in which no moth and rust can destroy (Matthew 6:20), usually surface after we've gone through trials, and survived what we see as terrible. It's God's ways, *not our own.*

3. *There's no past in the future.* This may be one of the most faith altering concepts to grasp because we have an enemy who'd like to continually convince us otherwise. Just as the woman at the well came to realize . . . her past, and how it was she

empty.

came to the well, didn't matter one bit when she met Jesus. It needed addressing, she needed a new direction, but she quickly moved forward with God's plan for her life—to spread the Good News.

When we're emptied, God can fill us. And when He fills us with His purposes and we're obedient to His plan, regardless of the cost, NOTHING can thwart that.

"For I am convinced that neither death nor life,
neither angels nor demons,
neither the present nor the future, nor any powers,
neither height nor depth, nor anything else
in all creation, will be able to separate us
from the love of God that is in Christ Jesus our Lord."
Romans 8:38-39 (NIV)

If God has forgiven you, as He promises He does through repentance, why can't you forgive yourself? If our sins are removed from us as far as the east is from the west to Him, why do they not seem that way to us?

"He has removed our sins
as far from us as the east is from the west."
Psalm 103:12 (NLT)

empty.

If we've confessed our sins, and if God chooses not to remember them, why do we?

"I, I am he who blots out your transgressions for my own sake, and I will not remember your sins."
Isaiah 43:25 (ESV)

We tend to forget that we're not alone, there's a spiritual realm that battles for our soul. In fact, it's in our emptiness that we believe a *lie* which works endlessly to convince us that we're empty: God doesn't love us, He's abandoned us, and life is being poured out in waste. We fail to realize that the enemy is constantly on the attack, and we lose sight of the battle we're continually in. It's not a fleshly battle—it's a spiritual one. Don't allow the enemy to fill your emptiness with lies.

You must allow God to go deep into your life, at the well, where you can be filled with the faith that you so desperately need to take this journey of life. But, we can find ourselves in a place of despair when we realize that God desires that His peace and joy would support us during times of pain and suffering, instead of eliminating it from our lives altogether. When the unthinkable happens, and God doesn't show up in the way we thought He should, it becomes our reason for dis-

empty.

couragement. Our perspective is warped through the ways of the world and we struggle to trust the ways of God.

We desperately try to find ways to rid ourselves of the pain we endure in this life and we become even more disillusioned. We believe the lies instead of the facts about faith, and we conclude that just standing still, doing nothing, depending on a God that doesn't seem to be showing up at all, seems senseless. We convince ourselves we must do *something*! We find ourselves moving ahead of God and then wondering why we can't find Him or why He's so far behind. We don't pray that our lives would conform and fulfill His will . . . we pray continually that He would approve our own.

But, what if we were completely convinced that our emptiness could radically change us? What if we were certain that the pain we are suffering is a pathway to a spiritual transformation that could potentially change the world? Quite possibly we'd be able to endure. Jesus did. It's because He knew the end result. He trusted God's plan and was committed to it regardless of the price. Listen, the power of the Gospel isn't its ability to generate a warm fuzzy feeling inside. If that's the purpose of the gospel, we as Christians

empty.

should be ashamed of it. But, if the message of the Gospel is the power to transform a life, bringing death to life, and resurrection that brings about eternal happiness for sinners who deserve to die, then we should not only NOT be ashamed of it, but we should be shouting it from the mountaintops. When we've met Jesus at the well, when we grasp Who He is and what He's done, we, just like the woman at the well, should be dropping our water jars and running to tell others of the Living Water that's available to them!

If we'll see the purpose for our emptiness for what it truly is, we'd see it as an opportunity to encounter God—we'd understand, clearly, that the more deeply we thirst . . . the more passionately we will pursue Living Water. The more clearly we see how it is that we're digging our own wells, the more fully we can repent of it and be transformed from the inside out. Our guilt and shame is in good hands with God. He knows what to do with it. Trust Him to diminish their power over you. Allow yourself to feel your disappointment, allow yourself to mourn over it all . . . and then allow God to fill you.

Know this: The extent to which you are emptied is proportional to the amount you can be filled. *It's a fact of faith.* Whether your glass is half

empty.

full or half empty, it must ALL be poured out so that it can be filled, *entirely.*

And don't believe the lie that faith wraps life up in a pretty package. *It doesn't.* There are no simple solutions, no easy answers, for life's toughest issues. In our emptiness, we're assured that God is the only one who has the answers. Only *He* understands our hurting hearts, empty lives, and searching souls. And although we'd like God to do things our way, *He doesn't.* We don't want God to comfort us *in* our troubles—we want Him to take them *from* us (2 Corinthians 1:4).

God's desire is to bring us to The Well and hear us say, in deepest desperation, *"Give me this water."* The emptiness you feel, that thirst that consumes your every thought is the very thing that is stirring your Spirit to draw back to God. It's God's way of showing you the measure of your faith. And faith is not illusive; God's not asking you to take a giant leap into the dark. Faith is trusting in God's Word, Living Water. And God knows what He's doing. He permits the emptiness in our lives *just when we need it most.* The woman's thirst brought her to the well at the precise moment that Jesus would be sitting there.

YOUR *emptiness is setting you up*
for a Divine appointment.

empty.

Living Water does more than quench your immediate thirst, it satisfies continually, enabling you to walk by faith, and allows you to gain a deeper perspective—understanding that you can expect God's blessings in spite of circumstances that give no evidence of them. Living Water allows you to tap into God's provision for every situation you face in life. And at that Well, we find Living Water waiting for us . . . *when we're thirsty.*

In our thirst, consumed by our emptiness, Living Water pours in,

"*Come, all you who are thirsty,*
come to the waters;
and you who have no money, come, buy and eat!
Come, buy wine and milk without money
and without cost."
Isaiah 55:1 (NIV)

and we find the Promise that we've been looking for:

"**Blessed** *are those who hunger and* **thirst**
for righteousness, for **they will be filled.**"
Matthew 5:6 (NLT)

Key words our souls cling to: *Blessed and Filled.*

empty.

Our thirst is slowly quenched, our emptiness steadily filled, when Revelation echoes Jesus' words within the depths of our soul:

"Come."
Let anyone who is thirsty come.
Let anyone who desires drink freely
from the water of life."
Revelations 22:17 (NLT)

Jesus beckons us to the Well when we're thirsty; yet too often, *we fail to come*. Instead, in our haste, we walk the other direction; often right into a desert. We fail to immerse ourselves into the Words of Jesus and the Promises of God because what we hear from Jesus and what we see lived out of the Christian faith in the Bible is so unlike what we know from our own experience. We're not convinced the whole thing will work for us. In fact, many of us have tried living life "by the Book," and things aren't "Blessed and Filled." In fact, it's quite the opposite—*empty*.

But the problem is that nothing stays empty for long. *Emptiness demands filling*. And unless we make a choice to go to the Well and fill ourselves with Living Water, we can be certain that our souls will demand the filling of everything that fails to satisfy.

empty.

The woman at the well had her life flash before her eyes and found her soul transformed by Jesus' simple, graceful, convicting words. Our lives can be transformed in the very same way. But we're going to have to find out what Jesus is saying to us. And He has something to say for EVERY-THING you're going through. He not only has a Word for you, He *is* The Word.

John the Apostle introduces Jesus as the Word, he gives us insight as to how the Word became flesh (John 1:1-5, 14, 18):

"In the beginning was the Word, and the Word was with God, and the Word was God. ² He was with God in the beginning. ³ Through him all things were made; without him nothing was made that has been made. ⁴ In him was life, and that life was the light of all mankind. ⁵ The light shines in the darkness, and the darkness has not overcome it.

¹⁴ *The Word became flesh and made his dwelling among us. We have seen his glory, the glory of the one and only Son, who came from the Father, full of grace and truth.*

¹⁸ *No one has ever seen God, but the one and only Son, who is himself God and is in closest relationship with the Father, has made him known."*

empty.

We have no question as to John's understanding of who Jesus was because Jesus Himself declares:

"Anyone who has seen me has seen the Father!"
John 14:9 (NLT)

The question is, *"Have you seen Him?"* Have you been to the Well? When's the last time you were there? Through an age old Hymn, "Speak, O Lord, Thy Servant Heareth," we see the essence of Living Water:

Speak, O Lord, Thy servant heareth,
To Thy Word I now give heed;
Life and spirit Thy Word beareth,
All Thy Word is true indeed.
Death's dread pow'r in me is rife;
Jesus, may Thy Word of Life
Fill my soul with love's strong fervor
That I cling to Thee forever.

Oh, what blessing to be near Thee
And to hearken to Thy voice;
May I ever love and fear Thee
That Thy Word may be my choice!
Oft were hardened sinners, Lord,
Struck with terror by Thy Word;
But to him who for sin grieveth
Comfort sweet and hope it giveth.

empty.

Lord, Thy words are waters living
Where I quench my thirsty need;
Lord, Thy words are bread life-giving,
On Thy words my soul doth feed.
Lord, Thy words shall be my light
Through death's vale and dreary night;
Yea, they are my sword prevailing
And my cup of joy unfailing.

Precious Jesus, I beseech Thee,
May Thy words take root in me;
May this gift from Heav'n enrich me
So that I bear fruit for Thee!
Take them never from my heart
Till I see Thee as Thou art,
When in heav'nly bliss and glory
I shall greet Thee and adore Thee.
—Anna Sophia of Hessen-Darmstadt, *Der Treue
Seelen-Freund Christus Jesus* (Jena, Germany: 1658)

God's Word is the product of His breath. It
gives life. We want to be filled and Jesus says
something that we must fully grasp:

*"The Spirit alone gives eternal life. Human effort ac-
complishes nothing. And **the very words I have spoken to you are spirit and life**."* (John 6:63 NLT)

---

empty.

It's His Word, staked on Who He is that we must fill our empty souls with. *It's the only thing that satisfies.* And His Word, spoken into our life, is useful, profitable, beneficial; it's used for teaching, refutation, convincing, persuading, correcting, and making things straight that were once crooked. We can also be certain that *it fills what is empty.*

First and foremost, the Word of God leads us to Jesus Himself. And then it transforms us. Our spiritual transformation takes place, our emptiness becomes filled with the Living Water that satisfies, when we go through the process of replacing lies with Truth. Jesus prayed for us in our emptiness. He knew what we needed in our emptiness:

"Make them holy by your truth; teach them your word, which is truth." (John 17:7 NLT)

We need a revelation from God to help us to see our lives through His eyes and not our own. And it's the Spirit of God that uses the Word of God to transform our lives and make us more like Jesus. And we need to understand that, no matter what the lies tell us, we are here, in this world, simply to understand Christ . . . *and for no other reason.* Our entire lives, just like the woman at the well, are lived for one purpose and one appointment—to encounter the Living God. Our whole

empty.

life's purpose is sealed up in the Word that God has spoken; and our fullness of faith will come in understanding that fact.

"All Scripture is breathed out by God and profitable for teaching, for reproof, for correction, and for training in righteousness, that the man of God may be complete, equipped for every good work." (2 Timothy 3:16-17 ESV)

Without God's Word, we would not exist. Your life is pointless, without God's purpose in it. And unless you're living out the purpose God created you for, you're *empty*.

You can't live without the Word of God, and if you are . . . whether you realize it or not . . . you're empty. It's His Word that is the spiritual nourishment you must have to live out your purpose and to be filled to the full . . . so that you *never* thirst.

Yet, in order to be filled with this Living Water, we need to learn a few things about how it works. It's not about quenching our thirst here and there. It's about staying connected to the Source of the Well. It's remaining at the Well. And one of the most recited and treasured Scriptures of all time turns our lives inside out as we need to more fully grasp it:

empty.

"But if you remain in me and my words remain in you, you may ask for anything you want, and it will be granted!" (John 15:7 NIV)

We're overjoyed by the second part of this verse, not so sure about the first. What does He mean? How can we claim such a promise, reaping its reward? We remain in Him and His Words remain in us when we:

1. *Accept the Word of God as Truth.* God's Word, the Bible, His Promises, must become the authority in our lives. It should be the compass we use for direction and our only counsel when making decisions. It should be used consistently and continually for everything we do in life. God has had the *first* Word to give us life, His Word should have the *last*.

It's God's Word that helps us to overcome the flaws of humanity caused by the Fall of mankind. In the midst of our pain and suffering, in the depths of our emptiness, we look to unreliable sources—we tend to rely on society, reason, and emotions. We're in desperate need of a standard that will not lead us astray. We need perfect instructions for this journey of life. And we find the wisdom of Solomon assuring us of what we need to know:

empty.

"Every word of God is flawless."

Proverbs 30:5 (NIV)

The Apostle Paul further explains the function of the Word of God in our lives (2 Timothy 3:16-17 NLT):

*"All Scripture is inspired by God and **is useful to teach us what is true and to make us realize what is wrong in our lives**. It corrects us when we are wrong and teaches us to do what is right. God uses it to prepare and equip his people to do every good work."*

The most important decision we can make in our lives is declaring the Word of God as the authority in our life. And everything we do and say should be filtered through it. We must resolve, by trusting in God's character, that we will trust Him at His Word, whether or not it makes sense to us, regardless if we "feel" like obeying it.

2. **Drink Deeply**. It's simply not enough to just "believe" the Bible. We must fill our minds with It to the point that our lives are transformed. We must read it, pray over it, and allow the Spirit to reveal God's heart through it, so that radical change can take place and we can be filled. It takes an accepting attitude—setting aside all pride.

empty.

James tells us the importance of a humble heart when receiving God's Word:

> "... *humbly* ***accept the word God***
> ***has planted in your hearts,***
> ***for it has the power***
> ***to save your souls.***"
> (James 1:21 NLT)

The Word, Jesus, has the power to save your soul. We must take a careful look at our lifestyle. How many hours are we watching television, reading fiction, and consuming time with various entertainment . . . in contrast to how much time we spend in God's Word. Digging deep tends to strike a nerve here. We wish God didn't dig in this particular spot. (We like that part of our life, we'd rather He not change things up.) But we fail to understand that it is in reading His Word, in connecting to Him, that we hear what we so desperately need to in our daily lives—*His voice.* God was clear on this:

"He must always keep that copy with him and read it daily as long as he lives. That way he will learn to fear the Lord his God by obeying all the terms of these instructions and decrees." (Deuteronomy 17:19 NLT)

empty.

We can envision that this might be God's first shovel full of dirt in our lives. Are we reading and learning from His Word every day? If we are, then we can be certain God is leading us—and if we're waiting on Him in faith, He's going to break His silence, and the flood waters will part—deliverance is assured—*it's only a matter of time*. Through His Word, we are promised that we will be filled to the point of being satisfied:

"But the truly happy people are those who carefully study God's perfect law that makes people free, and they continue to study it. They do not forget what they heard, but they obey what God's teaching says. Those who do this will be made happy." (James 1:25 NCV)

The benefits of drinking deeply of Living Water are endless. The Well doesn't bottom out—it's a wellspring.

3. *Never thirst.* We can read the Word, hear the Word, and never have it transform our lives. In order that we never thirst, we must pour out what has been poured in. James 1:22 (NLT) instructs us:

"But don't just listen to God's word. You must do what it says. Otherwise, you are only fooling yourselves."

empty.

We go back to the widow who filled jars with Olive oil. Had she merely heard what Elisha said and not done it, she would have never understood "The Empty Principle." She would have missed out on the miracle of God's abundant supply to fill the jars. If we don't drink deeply of the Living Water and then allow it to pour out of our lives, it's worthless. The blessings are in the pouring out. Jesus said (John 13:17 NLT):

"Now that you know these things, God will bless you for doing them."

The woman at the well heard what Jesus said and she dropped her water jar to tell others who He was. She did something with His Word.

There will be one vital question when we arrive at the Great Throne of God: "What did you do with Jesus?" What did we do with the revelation we were given of Him? How did we live our lives in Light of that Truth? Did we hoard it for ourselves, or share it freely with others? Did our lives give any evidence that we even met Jesus?—tough questions on a final exam that all of us will one day take.

We must allow the Living Water to fulfill its purpose in our lives. In the words of D.L. Moody:

empty.

"The Bible was not given to increase our knowledge but to change our lives."

The question is, "Has the Word of God, has the Bible, His Promises, Truth, changed *your* life?" If it has, then you might get thirsty, but you'll never thirst. Your emptiness may simply be because life is draining you dry and you need to go to the Well to drink more Living Water. Living Water washes, sanctifies, and cleanses the soul (Ephesians 5:26). It satisfies—*completely.* And it never fails, Jesus has promised:

"Whoever believes in me, as Scripture has said,
rivers of living water
will flow from within them."
John 7:38 (NIV)

Our emptiness crushes and presses us to the point of discovering that nothing but Living Water, Jesus Himself, satisfies.

Pressed out of measure and pressed to all length;
Pressed so intensely it seems, beyond strength;
Pressed in the body and pressed in the soul,
Pressed in the mind till the dark surges roll.
Pressure by foes, and a pressure from friends.
Pressure on pressure, till life nearly ends.

empty.

Pressed into knowing no helper but God;
Pressed into loving the staff and the rod.
Pressed into liberty where nothing clings;
Pressed into faith for impossible things.
Pressed into living a life in the Lord,
Pressed into living a Christ-life outpoured.
—Annie Johnson Flint

God has created you to have an undying thirst in your soul for Him and Him alone.

> **"None but God can satisfy the**
> **longings of an immortal soul;**
> **that as the heart was made for Him,**
> **so He only can fill it."**
> —Trench.

As you sit with Jesus at the well, you'll realize He wasn't all that thirsty—*but He knew you were.* And it wasn't your thirst that drew you to the well, it was Jesus Himself. At the Well, you'll discover that in your emptiness, in your desperate attempts to be satisfied, God wants you settling for nothing less than the *fullness* He gives . . . He wants you to draw near to Him, The Well—and He beckons you with love,

"Come, drink, and live."

empty.

If you need directions to get to The Well,
visit: http://www.ScriptureNow.com,
and it's there where you'll find Living Water.

BONUS FEATURE:

1st Chapter of

BE STILL

Let Jesus Calm Your Storms

Cherie Hill

BE STILL

Let Jesus Calm Your Storms

Cherie Hill

Praise for *Be Still*

"With this detailed study of the incident of Jesus calming the storm, Cherie Hill has not only brought new light to a familiar Gospel story, she has showed us how to both weather and grow from our personal storms. *Be Still* is a healing balm to the soul. My best advice — get this book, use it, and buy another one for your best friend!" — Jim Thomson, M.A., LCPC, author and speaker.

"*Be Still* is a wealth of Scripture that readers can return to again and again for encouragement in the midst of trials. *Be Still* is not a book that you read once, put on your bookshelf, and then forget about. It's a book that doesn't promise quick fixes, or endless sunshine. Instead, it is a lifeline attached to God's Word, designed to help the reader find peace in the midst of each and every storm that comes their way." — Deborah Porter, writer, editor, and radio talk show host.

"*Be Still — Let Jesus Calm Your Storms* combines intellectual common sense, Biblical scriptures, and an author dedicated to helping people who have suffering in their lives. If you are currently going through a storm, this book can definitely help you through it. Buy a copy for yourself, buy a copy for a friend, or leave a copy somewhere for a stranger." — Dan Blankenship, author of *The Running Girl*.

"The book nicely bridges the gap between those who doubt God because there are storms and the true lessons to be drawn from those storms. One of the best parts of this book is the way the author explores creating both inner and outer peace. Many people are more troubled in their minds than they are in reality; this book can help." —Donald M. Mitchell, Amazon.com top 10 Reviewer, Harvard Graduate, author, and CEO featured in *Forbes Magazine*.

"*Be Still, Let Jesus Calm Your Storms*, by Cherie Hill, is an inspiring book that Christians, as well as all individuals who are seeking peace in a chaotic world, will find to be 'life-changing.' Regardless of where readers are in their walk with God, the words of the author and her use of Scripture to support her advice and encouragement will enable them to understand much more about faith and how it is the path that gives peace of mind in all situations." —Bettie Corbin Tucker, Publisher, IP book reviewer, former radio talk show host, and published author.

"I can highly recommend this book to anyone who is looking for a fulfilling life purpose. Cherie Hill's greatest accomplishment is making a difference in the lives of people who are in need of human caring, a few warm words of encouragement and an open heart." —Rebecca Johnson, Amazon.com top 10 Reviewer.

BE STILL

Let Jesus Calm Your Storms

Cherie Hill

This book is dedicated to God . . .

the *perfect author* of my life.

My greatest joy is just in "knowing" You.

Thank you for teaching me to "*Be Still.*"

Most of all, thank you for loving me enough

to use my life according to *Your* purposes.

Contents

Preface

I would like to take a moment to explain exactly how this book was inspired and why I believe it can deeply change your life.

As a born again Christian, I began asking God to give my life purpose and fill me in a way that the world could not. I needed something that was eternal and meaningful. And well, God answered me. I believe that God has always had a plan for me, yet it was only when I finally reached out to Him that He revealed His purpose for my life. God began to show me all of the "spiritual gifts" that He had given to me. He gave me insight as to how all of my life experiences had strengthened and developed those gifts.

You see, I have always been a good listener. For some reason, people have always felt more than comfortable revealing their most intimate problems in their lives to me. I never understood why complete strangers would open up and express their deepest pains and "storms" of life, while looking to me for some type of answer. Many times, I found myself overwhelmed with empathy, yet filled with sorrow because I was unable to provide answers or even point them in the right direction. When God finally revealed His plan for my life, I began to see the whole picture come together. God had a vision for my life . . . and it was in my moment of surrender that He gave me eyes to see.

God began to teach me how critical Scripture is to our lives; His Word has become the very breath that gives me life. His plan for me was to lead others to Jesus by simply providing them with Scriptures that would speak directly to their circumstances. It is in receiving God's grace that we can live with confident hope – it is His Word that gives us the faith we need to receive that grace. It really is the Truth that sets us free and fills us with hope. His Word produces a faith in us that will never fail.

And so, to make a long story short, God revealed "ScriptureNow.com" to me. I can honestly tell you that it has been the greatest blessing in my life and in the lives of hundreds of thousands of people in over 30 countries around the world. I can't imagine one day of my life going by without reaching out and sharing the Word of God to people in this way! And God did all of this in the midst of my raging storms of life.

This is where "Be Still" took on its purpose . . . as I have read the countless prayer requests through ScriptureNow.com, God spoke to me and showed me the miracle of "Jesus Calms the Storm" in a whole new light. This miracle goes to the heart of every single situation that we face in life, and I believe God filled me with the wisdom and insight to be able to write this book for you.

I hope that this book touches your heart and speaks to you through its message. I pray that you will always draw close to God, so that He can comfort, encourage, and rescue you through all of life's storms. I pray that you will also visit me at: http://www.ScriptureNow.com *and experience a great blessing in your life!*

Testimonies from ScriptureNow.com

Oh, what a blessing . . . I am so thankful to God that I found your website. God speaks to me through you.

Thank you for your Scriptures, they seem to always come on time.

Thank you! It's amazing how the Scriptures have gone in line with what I am dealing with!!

Thank you so much for your never ending help in my life. The Scriptures were helpful, powerful, and effective in my life.

You have helped save my life. My crisis is over and God gave me a miracle!

God bless you mightily for your compassionate ministry.

I don't know how you knew, but this Scripture was exactly what I needed. Thank you!!!

Thank you. This is what I needed to hear!

Thank you for all of your prayers and love over this year and for being a safe place to call out to. I can't tell you just how much the daily Scriptures have blessed my heart.

You know, before I found out about ScriptureNow.com, I was not lost, but not headed in the right direction.

I will never be able to express the power I have experienced in the Scriptures that you send.

You will never fully understand how God has used your website to turn my life around and get me moving in the right direction.

I had lost all hope until I found your website, and now I am filled with a hope I have never felt before.

The nine Scriptures that you sent have given me nine days of strength. I had never experienced God speaking to me until now. Thank you for using His Word to help me hear Him.

I look so forward to receiving your Daily Scripture. It just seems as though God is speaking right through it!

You will never quite understand the impact your Ministry is having.

Thank you from the bottom of my heart for your prayers and your concerns. I don't think I could have coped with the pressures I have found myself under if it would not have been for your caring and sending me Scripture and prayer. I now know that I will overcome through Christ!

May God richly bless you for the work you are doing for Him.

I'm wondering if this is really God's email . . . the Scriptures you send speak so directly to me . . . that it must be.

Introduction

The Storm

Do you feel as though you're in a raging storm? Storms of life flood your spirit with disillusionment, despair, and disappointment. The consuming waves of a storm in life can submerge your soul with agonizing fear. When you're in a storm of life, it feels as though each breath might be your last. The ongoing destruction from the storm forces you to cling to anything and everything, in the hopes of somehow surviving it all. As the storm continues to rage, you suddenly realize that there's no lifeboat—there's no quick escape. You're on your own. Usually, very quickly, the terror sets in; with it comes despair and hopelessness. The desperation that overcomes you, suddenly, becomes more than you can withstand. As the end seems to be drawing nearer, with each moment that passes, all you can do is stand by and watch it all unfold.

Our storms of life bring us to the point where we realize that we have nowhere to go, but to God. In a moment of overwhelming desperation, when we finally do call out to Him, we suddenly realize that our relationship with Him has grown cold. Through our cries for help, without stable ground to stand on, it's anger that takes over and we shout, *"Lord, don't you care?"*

We've all been there, at one time or another. If you haven't experienced a storm in your life, then praise God; but, get ready because Jesus assured us:

> *I have told you all this so that you*
> *may have peace in me.*
> *Here on earth you will have many*
> *trials and sorrows.*
> *But take heart, because I have overcome the world.*
> (John 16:33 NLT)

The Controversy of the Miracle

The miracle of "Jesus Calms the Storm" has been called one of the most controversial miracles that Jesus performed. Even today, we witness those who are pronounced dead . . . receive life again, blind who against all odds see, illnesses that are cured without explanation, and tragic accidents where miraculously people survive. We witness miracles every day and realize that they are from the power of something far greater than what we can comprehend.

Yet, even in the face of such miracles, we allow human reasoning to get the best of us. Doubt, more often than not, wins out. We end up walking by sight, instead of by faith. So, we wrestle with our faith, just as the Disciples did on the Sea of Galilee.

The battle begins . . . *within*. How do we accept someone controlling the wind and the waves in a violent storm? Even if we want to believe, this kind of miracle pushes our faith a little farther than we'd like. This kind of faith presses us beyond our comfort zone.

We like to keep God in a box. We're comfortable with Him in some things in our lives, but not others. We're content in keeping Him where we've put Him . . . allowing Him out of the box is just too risky — we're not sure what to expect from Him. We're not convinced He'll do things the *way* they should be done or in the *timing* that they should be done. We believe that it's possible for Him to heal someone we're praying for, but we're just not certain that He can do anything in *our* situation. We're convinced that there are just some things that God is either too busy to deal with, or He just really doesn't care. It has been said that to ask God for help in "small things" is wasting His time—be assured, *ALL things are small to God.* He is looking to and fro the earth for someone to not only call out to Him, but to *believe Him* (2 Chronicles 16:9).

He is looking for *your* faith *in the midst of your storms of life.* He has allowed the storm, in an effort to increase your faith, *by threatening to destroy it.* Out of His great love for you, He calls out to you through your storm and asks, *"Who do you say I am"* (Matthew 16:15)? As your life is pushed to the edge, His voice calls down from heaven . . . demanding an answer.

It is your answer that determines whether or not you will make it through the storm and if there will be anything left in the aftermath. It is your faith in God that makes *all* the difference. Trust Him, and cling to your faith . . . God ALWAYS keeps His Word.

According to your faith
and trust and reliance
[on the power invested in Me]
be it done to you;
(Matthew 9:29 AMP)

This miracle is for you to understand
the purpose of the storms in your life
and how to persevere through them.
By applying this miracle to your life,
you will find that God can calm
all of your storms . . .
if you will just have faith that He can.

The miracle in the storm on the Sea of Galilee revealed the Disciples' lack of faith in Jesus as the Son of God. Although they had witnessed Jesus perform many miracles, they still had doubt about who He really was. It was through this miracle that their faith was truly put to the test. The Disciples believed, just as most people did, that many miracles are understandably possible, *but only God* could control the wind and the waves. There was no doubt in their minds that this kind of power could only come from the hand of God. God's desire is to move His hand in your storms, as well. *He is looking for your faith.*

What you must understand is that this miracle was not just a story of God's awesome power — it was not just another miracle. This miracle was for you to understand the purpose of the storms in *your* life and how to persevere through them. By applying this miracle to your life, you will find that God can calm all of your storms . . . *if you will just have faith that He can.*

Storms Will Come

After receiving thousands of emails from people all over the world through the ScriptureNow.com Ministry, I might guess that your storms are a broken relationship, a shattered marriage, depression, despair over unsaved loved ones, job anxiety, unemployment, financial failure, an illness, death, or some unexpected tragedy. Maybe you feel that life in general is a raging storm. No matter how big or small your storm, you feel that no one seems to understand; you're convinced that you're in the boat alone. With each agonizing moment that passes, you feel that you're one day closer to drowning; it seems as though nothing and no one can save you.

If you aren't currently in a storm, be on the lookout. The enemy is looking for an opportunity to send the perfect storm into your life. He is well aware of our deepest desires and our innermost struggles. Satan not only attacks us where we are weakest; more often, he attacks in those areas where we feel we are strongest. He knows exactly where pride exists. He knows we won't see an attack coming when we're overly confident in a particular area of our lives. He knows those places in our lives where we've decided to play God and we've shut God out. He's able to see any crack we leave in the doorway, and He feels more than comfortable letting himself in. The enemy is always at work, and he is more than willing to kick you while you're down. He's not particularly concerned about what's going on in your life and whether or not the timing is convenient. He's simply out to destroy your faith in God. The enemy's attacks are deceitful and destructive — you won't even see what's coming. Just as in the miracle of Jesus Calms the Storm, many times, the storms of our lives will come from out of nowhere — *unexpectedly.*

Faith isn't faith,
unless it believes in the unseen.
It doesn't take faith
at all to cling to what you see.
Faith in God trusts Him even when you can't see
the very next step in front of you.

How many times have we judged others and said, "I'd never do that. That could never happen to me . . . I'm too loving, too giving, too faithful, too loyal, too obedient, too prayerful, too dedicated to God. Besides, I go to church on Sunday!" Before we know it, we find ourselves in the midst of that *very* storm; we're dazed and confused, wondering how we got there and how to get out.

The Storm Has Great Purpose

The Disciples were not exempt from a test of faith and neither are we. God's purposes for them were so great, so critical to His plans, that He allowed a raging storm to take over their boat on the Sea of Galilee—bringing them to the edge of their faith. He increased their faith by asking them to step into a boat and *risk it*.

Faith isn't faith, unless it requires taking a step into the unseen. It doesn't take faith at all to cling to what you see. The faith that God is after is a faith that clings to Him and isn't threatened or destroyed by adversity and uncertainty. You know that you have genuine faith when common sense tells you to stop believing, but you continue to trust God anyway. *It's all about your faith in God—*

don't ever believe otherwise.

This unexpected storm tested these men, who considered themselves *very* skilled fishermen, so that their faith would be strengthened for the journey ahead. In their weakness, they realized they were helpless without their Savior. When Jesus performed the incredible miracle of calming the storm, it caused these expert fishermen, who had been through many storms on this Sea, to experience a storm that would bring them to the end of themselves. Although the Disciples were master fishermen, God took the area of the Disciples' lives where they felt most confident . . . and tested them. God knew they needed to be brought to the end of their own abilities, so that they would trust in His.

Rest assured, God is bringing you to your knees, so that you can witness His hand lift you up. The message that God needed the Disciples to understand was that it was *by faith alone* that they could be saved. It's the message He wants *you* to know, as well.

But people are declared righteous
because of their faith,
not because of their work.
(Romans 4:5 NLT)

By sending the storm and testing them in it, God turned these men into the greatest witnesses for Christ that the world has ever known. Our storms will also come in those areas where we least expect them.

Don't be deceived,
God has allowed the storm in your life . . .
with a plan to use it ALL
for your good and HIS glory!

Our pride will keep us from seeing the storms coming. It is in the areas where pride exists that Satan sees an easy target. Don't be deceived . . . God *allowed* the storm in this miracle, and He's allowing it in your life . . . with a plan to use it ALL for *your good* and His glory!

Then the Lord asked Satan, 'Have you noticed my servant Job? He is the finest man in all the earth — a man of complete integrity. He fears God and will have nothing to do with evil.' Satan replied to the Lord, 'Yes, Job fears God, but not without good reason! You have always protected him and his home and his property from harm. You have made him prosperous in everything he does. Look how rich he is! But take away everything he has, and he will surely curse you to your face!' 'Alright, you may test him,' the Lord said to Satan. 'Do whatever you want with everything he possesses, but don't harm him physically.' So Satan left the Lord's presence. (Job 1:8-12 NLT)

Never doubt that there are spiritual conversations about *you*. Yes, *you*! You are known by name in the heavenly realms, and we know this from Isaiah 45:3 (NLT):

> *I am the Lord, the God of Israel,*
> *the one who calls you by name.*

You are no different than Job or the Disciples, in that, God will only allow those things which He knows will bring you closer to Him, give Him the glory, and make your heart more like His. It is imperative to truly understand that God will never give you more than you can withstand, and He will always make a way through your storms when you trust in Him.

> *But remember that the temptations that come*
> *into your life are no different from what others experi-*
> *ence. And God is faithful. He will keep the temptation*
> *from becoming so strong that you can't stand up*
> *against it. When you are tempted, he will show you a*
> *way out so that you will not give into it.*
> (1 Corinthians 10:13 NLT)

When you feel that God has allowed your storms, you should be comforted in just knowing that God alone is control of them. In your storms of life, your spirit can be quieted by grabbing hold of the Truth: If God has allowed a storm . . . *He will make a way through it.*

If God has allowed the storm,
He will make a way through it.
Be certain that God is only allowing the storm
because He knows the blessing behind it.
Through the storm, God is giving
you the opportunity to experience,
first hand, His miraculous and sufficient
power in your life.

He has assured you that He is with you *always* (Matthew 28:20). You should feel secure, in just knowing, that God has set the boundaries and perimeters of your storm—just as he did with Job. It should strengthen you to know that God is allowing this storm only because He knows the blessing behind it.

When God is at work in your life, you will often experience the miraculous and sufficient power of God in your storms . . . *even more than in your times of great blessings.* We can only truly appreciate the glory of being on the mountaintop when we've had to climb up from the valley. And the only way from one mountaintop to the next is *through* the valleys. It's in the valley where the richest soil in the world is found . . . *God knows what He's doing when He's growing your faith.*

It is only through the storms that you will truly know the heart of God. In your storms, you've been given the opportunity to encounter God — the choice to accept His invitation is yours.

As long as we insist on being in control, God will not interfere. He will allow us to go our own way, until we come to a place of surrender. In order to experience God's miracles in our lives, we must be willing to relinquish control, and let *God be God.*

Too often, instead of trusting in God's sovereign purpose in our storms, many of us feel anger. We feel like God allowed us to walk into the storm or that He even led us right into it. We're convinced that He could have spared us the pain and suffering. Understanding the purpose of your storms will help you persevere through them and bring you closer to God, instead of casting your soul deeper into despair by allowing your heart to become hardened in your distress.

In all this, Job did not sin by blaming God.
(Job 1:22 NLT)

(If you have not read the book of Job . . . I challenge you to do so and understand what it truly
means to have faith in God through the most tragic storms of life.)

Why A Storm?

We live in a world filled with anxiety and tremen-
dous uncertainty. Each and every day we are confronted by stories that shake the foundation of our
faith—to a point of near destruction. If we, personally, aren't facing unthinkable trials and tragedies, we worry about friends and family members
who are facing the inconceivable. Or we become
fearful of what *lies ahead* in our lives.

Jesus performs many miracles
in our storms of life —
showing us that He is ALL we need,
when there is a need, is just one of them.

We wonder what *good* could possibly come from such overwhelming anxiety and fear. But, it's in the worst of times that we find the most opportune moment to re-examine our lives. What have we taken for granted? What are our morals and values? On what have we built our foundation and will it be able to withstand the storms in our lives? In the storms of life, we have two choices: we can reaffirm the faith we embraced when we accepted Christ into our life, or we can walk away.

For those who have never known Jesus, these times of suffering are an opportunity for the heart to be opened and the need for God to surface. God is at work, even when we are unaware. The storms convince us that we're lost and in need of help. In our desperation, we realize that we need a "compass."

When you're holding a compass, you can turn your feet in any direction, but the arrow of the compass will faithfully point to Magnetic North. If you should ever become lost, the compass will give you an indication of where you are and where you're going. In life, "North" is Christ. We may take a path that leads us in the "world's" direction and we might get lost along the way; but, when we turn to Christ, He realigns our lives in the direction of God's will. Jesus performs many miracles in our storms of life — showing us that He is all that we need, when there is a need, is just one of them.

Whether you're a person of faith in God, or a person still questioning and seeking answers, it's likely that you're open-minded to miracles. If you don't need a miracle right now, you probably know someone who does. You see, God does extraordinary things for ordinary people. He loves to surprise us with His goodness and His power, in order to help us in our most desperate times. He can do anything. But, in the storms of your life, He wants you to know His presence, so that as you wait for His perfect timing, you can be filled with hope. He wants you to find security and peace in His care; He wants you trusting that He is mighty to save (Zephaniah 3:17).

If you want to find an extraordinary miracle in the life of an ordinary man, you need to look no further than to Moses. Moses was traveling in the desert when God spoke to him through a burning bush. (If you want to get an amazing glimpse of God's awesome power, you should make it a priority to read through the book of Exodus.) God caught Moses off-guard, in the middle of the desert, through a burning bush. His encounter with God was life-altering. This miracle enabled Moses to walk forward in faith, trusting God, because he could not deny such a supernatural occurrence. Moses was able to walk through even greater adversity along his journey because with each step of faith that he took . . . God strengthened his faith through one miracle after another.

---

*Our storms come with an objective
that is far more significant
than our present need for comfort.
God is doing us a favor, by bringing
us to a place of forfeiting
our will in our lives,
so that we will embrace His.*

God used a burning bush to initially get Moses' *attention*; then, when Moses came to examine the bush further, *God called out his name.* (In our storms of life . . . God calls out our name, too. He wants our undivided attention.) As Moses drew even closer to God, God stopped him and told him to take off his shoes because he was standing on holy ground. He wanted Moses to know that he was in the presence of Almighty God. He wanted him to remember that moment *forever.* That event is now remembered thousands of years later — God's miracle made its mark on history.

In this particular miracle, God didn't stop with a burning bush. He goes on to tell Moses that He has heard the cries of His people in their suffering, and He has come down to save them. In your storms of life, God wants to step in and give you a miracle, too. But, it's less about the actual miracle and more about your encounter with Him. He wants to give you the faith that will see you through the storms of your life that are yet to come. *And they will come.*

The poet Elizabeth Barrett Browning once, famously, wrote that *"Earth is crammed full of heaven, and every common bush aglow with God. Those who see . . . take off their shoes."* God wants to bring *you* to a place of "taking off *your* shoes."

This miracle on the Sea of Galilee, this storm, was preparing the Disciples' faith for the journey ahead.

It was the storm that would bring them to their knees and really get their attention. God also knows exactly what storms you and I will need to go through, in order to draw us closer to Him. Our storms come with an objective that is far more significant than our present need for comfort. God is doing us a favor by bringing us to a place of forfeiting all of our expectations in our lives, so that we will embrace His. Your storms can create the greatest intimacy between yourself and God. There is *nothing* more awesome. When you're walking with God, the emptiness and loneliness that daily consumes your soul is filled with a joy that overflows and a peace that is beyond all understanding.

Rest assured that God can perform
miracles in your life,
in your storms,
just as He did when He calmed
the Sea of Galilee.
The question is,
"Do YOU believe He can?"

This miracle was not just for the Disciples—it was for *you*. You will experience a miracle in your life, if you will understand how significant the storms of your life are to your faith. You must realize that God can do ANYTHING—He *can* calm the storm. But, what He really wants to do is use your life for His purposes—something far greater than anything you could dare ask for or imagine

(Ephesians 3:20). He wants to give you something far more fulfilling than you could ever desire.

It should be encouraging to know that if God could take these few ordinary men and use this storm to change the world forever through their testimony . . .

He can use your storms for His glory, too.

**God is strengthening our faith
in the storms of our lives,
and He wants us to get
the message loud and clear—
our faith is not strengthened
by striving after it,
but by resting in Him, the Faithful One.**

Yes, God wants to use *you*. Rest assured He can perform miracles in your life, in your storms, just as He did when He calmed the Sea of Galilee. The question is, "Do *you* believe He can?"

*Then Jesus told him,
"You believe because you have seen me.
Blessed are those who haven't seen me
and believe anyway."*
(John 20:29 NLT)

"What do you mean, 'If I can'?" Jesus asked. "Anything is possible if a person believes" (Mark 9:23 NLT).

God intends to perform a miracle in your life and not have you say, *"How did He do that?"* Instead, He wants for you to have the same experience as the Disciples of Jesus had—it was in their awe and amazement that they asked, *"Who is this man, that even the winds and waves obey him?"*

And they were filled with awe amazement. They said to one another 'Who is this man, that even the winds and waves obey him?' (Luke 8:25 NLT)

God desires for you to be in such awe and amazement of His power that you are less concerned about how He did it, but rather, *who* it is that did it! We beg and beg for miracles in our lives, constantly wondering why God won't do something; yet, when He does, He mystifies us even more. It's our heart He's after, and He's more than willing to bring about a miracle in your life in order to capture it. His miracle for you is that you will not be overcome by your storms, but that you will know Who to come to when your storms emerge. He's strengthening your faith in Him *through* the storms. He wants us to get the message loud and clear: Our faith is not strengthened by striving after it, but by resting in Him, *the Faithful One.*

God knows what He's doing.
Let the storms come, and let the waters rise —
God is taking you deeper

Just as in the Sea of Galilee, God knows our storms often come from out of nowhere. He's well aware that when they do . . . we're likely to go into shear panic. His miracle for you, in the storm, is that you can be at rest with Him through your faith.

We look at the storms of our lives and too often, ask, *"If God is so loving, why does He allow pain and suffering in my life? What have I done to deserve being a victim in this circumstance? Why do I need to go through this storm? Why can't He just take me around it? I want out and NOW!"* The truth is, God knows us . . . He knows what it will take to bring us to our knees. It is upon our knees where we learn to walk by faith and receive the peace that only He can provide when storms arise. Remember this clearly: ANYTHING that drops us to our knees and brings us to the foot of the Cross is

GOOD for us. In our moments of complete brokenness, when the flesh is weak, but the spirit is willing (Matthew 26:41), He wants us to know: *In Jesus* we will find confident patience, strength, endurance, and peace.

God knows exactly what we need, in order to make it through this journey of life. At times, our journey will take us into unfamiliar, intimidating, territory . . . which may be exactly where God wants us, so that He can perform His greatest work in our lives.

If we go back to the book of Exodus, and the life of Moses, we find that when Pharaoh finally let the people go, God did not lead them along the main road that ran through the territory—*even though that was the shortest route to the Promised Land.* Here's what He said, *'If the people are faced with a battle, they might change their minds and return to Egypt.' So God led them in a round-about way through the wilderness toward the Red Sea.* (Exodus 13:17-18 NLT) You see, God may have led them the long way, but He was preparing an even greater miracle than Him *rescuing* them.

You might be tempted to believe that God doesn't know what He's doing—that He's causing you to endure unnecessary pain and suffering. But, rest assured, God knows exactly what He's doing. Let the storms come, and let the waters rise — *God is taking you deeper.*

God knows that this won't be the last storm you will encounter in your life. It's a fallen world; He wants to build your faith in Him, so when the sea rages and the storm clouds begin closing in…you will find peace in Him.

Don't worry about anything; instead pray about everything. Tell God what you need, and thank him for all he has done. If you do this, you will experience God's peace, which is far more wonderful than the human mind can understand. His peace will guard your hearts and minds as you live in Christ Jesus.
(Philippians 4:6-7 NLT)

Faith Can Calm the Storm

Through God's Word, we are assured that He can calm the "external" storm; but, the storm He really wants to calm is the one *inside* of you — the "internal" storm. Ask yourself, while reading through this miracle, "Was Jesus just simply telling the wind and the waves, *'Peace! Be Still!'*? Or was there a deeper message?" Jesus was speaking to

YOU in this miracle. You see, it took no effort at all for Jesus to calm the external, physical, storm. It was much more important for Him to teach us how to calm the storm within us — the "spiritual" storm.

God wants you in the back
of the boat with Jesus —
a place of peace and rest.
He wants you to "Be Still";
yet, we find that "being still"
requires action . . .
it demands your faith.

When you learn how to calm the storm within, through your faith in God, the wind and the waves may be threatening to take you under, but you will find yourself in the eye of the storm...*at peace.*

We can look at a hurricane as being symbolic to our storms of life. Hurricanes have a distinctive feature called an "eye." The eye of a hurricane is in the middle of the spiral of the storm. The eye is produced by the spiraling action of the storm, and it is the area where the air is slowly sinking. When the eye of a hurricane passes over an area, the winds decrease to a gentle breeze and the rain stops. In the eye of the hurricane, you may even be able to see the sun during the day or the stars out at night. Then, as the rest of the storm passes and the wind suddenly changes directions, the storm becomes ferocious again.

God wants you to be in the eye of your storms in life. In the eye, He knows that you will be able to see the light of day and enjoy the beauty of the stars at night. In the eye of storm, the winds and waters may rage around you, but you will be experiencing peace in the midst of it. God has given us His Word, the Scriptures, to keep us from being overcome by the most powerful winds that reside just outside the eye wall of the storm.

Understanding the miracle of "Jesus Calms the Storm" makes us certain of one thing: Whatever the storm is, however fierce, and however the storm came about, God can calm it. The question is, "Will *you* have faith that God can calm *your* storm?" The lesson in this fantastic miracle of "*Jesus Calms the Storm*" is to have confident faith in God and get to the back of the boat with Jesus — a place of peace and rest. What we also learn through this miracle is that "*Being Still,*" actually, requires action. Let the miracle of Jesus calming the storm increase your faith and bring about a miracle in *your life,* by teaching you to "*Be Still.*"

NOTE TO READER: *I encourage you to go through this book and highlight the Scriptures. When you only have a moment, skim through the book and be encouraged!*

*Also, don't miss the section in the back of this book, "**God's Word On** . . ." Use the section as a reference to God's Promises that will encourage your faith through all your storms of life.*

Chapter1

⚓ Understanding the Storm ⚓

Jesus Calms the Storm

On that day, when evening had come, he said to them, "Let us go across to the other side." And leaving the crowd, they took him with them in the boat, just as he was. And other boats were with him. And a great windstorm arose, and the waves were breaking into the boat, so that the boat was already filling. But he was in the stern, asleep on the cushion. And they woke him and said to him, "Teacher, do you not care that we are perishing?" And he awoke and rebuked the wind and said to the sea, "Peace! Be Still!" And the wind ceased, and there was a great calm. He said to them, "Why are you so afraid? Have you still no faith? (Mark 4:35-40 ESV)

Then Jesus asked, "Where is your faith?" And they were filled with awe and amazement. They said to one another, "Who is this man, that even the winds and waves obey him?" (Luke 8:25 NLT)

In order to understand the miracle of "Jesus Calms the Storm," we must first understand the power of the sea; what its power represented then and now. According to the Gospels, Jesus' ministry was centered around the Sea of Galilee. While many important events occurred in Jerusalem, Jesus spent most of His ministry along the shore of this freshwater lake. It was there that Jesus gave more than half of His parables and where He performed most of His miracles.

The Sea of Galilee was known for its sudden, violent storms. When it raged, the threat of drowning among fisherman was all too real. The Sea of Galilee is unique in that it is seven hundred feet below sea level, making it the lowest freshwater lake on the earth. At its widest point, the lake measures thirteen miles from north to south and seven and a half miles from east to west. Its deepest point is estimated at around two hundred feet.

The Sea's location was significant because it made the Sea susceptible to the sudden and violent storms. The storms would often develop when an east wind dropped cool air over the warm air rising from the Sea. This change produced well known furious storms, without warning.

Never forget that God is in control.
The question is, "When a storm arises,
will you cry out to the only
One who can help you?"

The word "sea," in Hebrew, comes from the name of the evil god in the Babylonian creation story. It meant "evil" and "a mysterious and threatening force opposed to God." When Hebrews wanted to declare God's authority, they spoke of His power over the sea. In Psalms 89:9 (NKJV), the Psalmist said,

> *You rule the raging of the sea,*
> *when its waves rise, you still them.*

In Psalm 107:23-30 (NLT), we not only find a prophecy of "Jesus Calms the Storm," but an acknowledgement of God's power over the storms.

Some went off in ships, plying the trade routes of the world. They too, observed the Lord's power in action, his impressive works on the deepest seas. He spoke, and the winds rose, stirring up the waves. Their ships were tossed to the heavens and sank again to the depths; the sailors cringed in terror. They reeled and staggered like drunkards and were at wits' end. "Lord, help!" they cried in their trouble, and he saved them from their distress. He calmed the storm to a whisper and stilled the waves. What a blessing was that stillness as he brought them safely into the harbor!

As powerful as storms were and still are today, God is acknowledged to have power over them all. Never forget this truth in your own life: *God is in control.* The question is, "When a storm arises, will you cry out to the *One* who can help you?"

It was known that storms on this Sea could arise from nowhere; so, since Jesus was the Son of God, one might think that *surely* He knew there would be a great storm on this venture across the Sea. And if this were so, why did He choose to take His Disciples into it? You would almost expect, since Jesus was with the Disciples on this trip across the Sea, they would be free from worry. We can be certain they didn't expect to encounter a raging storm that they may have experienced on many other trips.

Certainly, the Disciples who gave up everything in life and obediently followed Jesus would be protected from harm's way. They might even expect that this would be the most wonderful venture across the Sea that they had ever experienced. They more than likely found confidence in their commitment to Jesus and felt secure in His ability to protect them. They loved Jesus, believed in Him, and left behind everything in life to follow Him; yet, the Disciples' devotion did nothing to protect them from the terror of this storm.

In the Boat

Many times, we as Christians feel the same way the Disciples did . . . when we become a Christian and accept Jesus as Lord and Savior, shouldn't we be protected? We, understandably, *assume* that life should be "easier"; we feel certain that we should instantly have a closer relationship with God. We can falsely believe that we no longer have to endure "storms" in our lives. But, then, suddenly, one day, in one moment in time, we're faced with the painful truth—*it's not the way it works*. Our false expectations can create a storm in and of itself. When life doesn't happen just as we think it should, the winds start roaring and the storm clouds look ferocious. Our faith can begin to fail amidst the overwhelming atmosphere of doubt and despair.

When we make a stand in our faith, when we decide to get into the boat with Jesus, Satan unleashes his rage against us. We are now "officially" his enemy, and the true battle has begun. Shockingly, as we take each step of faith, our storms seem to actually come *more often* than *before* we believed!

When we're faced with the storms that we must endure, when walking with God, we find ourselves in the midst of our storm crying out, *"Why is this happening to me? If You're a God of love, why all this pain? Why do the innocent suffer? If You're a God of order, why all the chaos? If You're so powerful, why do You seem so incapable? By the way, where are You?"* It is at this time that we need to be reminded of the Truth: Jesus told us in John 16:33 (NLT):

> *I have told you all this*
> *so that you may have peace in me.*
> *Here on earth you will have many*
> *trials and sorrows.*
> *But take heart,*
> *because I have overcome the world.*

When you're in the boat with Jesus, the answers to your questions come in many *unexpected* ways. *Sometimes*, they come by way of a storm that threatens to take you under. You see, instead of presenting just an "ordinary" trial with an "ordinary storm," the storm in this miracle would be like no other. This storm would threaten to take the Disciples' very lives. This storm would ultimately test their faith. This miracle would cause the Disciples to ask, "*Who is this man?*"

Jesus didn't come to get you out of the storms in your life —
He came to take you through them.

It's interesting that the most violent storm these fishermen had ever experienced was when Jesus, the Son of God, was in the boat with them. It should be comforting to know that in the most violent storms of your life . . . *Jesus is in the boat with you, too.*

Understanding the storms of your life is realizing that although the waves may start crashing in on you . . . *Jesus is with you.* More importantly, you must be assured through His Word: He will not allow you to perish, if you will acknowledge His presence in your life and call out His name. Surely, your boat cannot go down with the Son of God in it! Don't be deceived, Jesus didn't come to get you out of the storms in your life—He came to take you *through* them.

In the storms of your life,
God is always at work—
drawing you closer to Him and weaving
all of your paths into His purposes.

You see, God knew that the Disciples needed to go from "here" to "there," in order to experience the miracle. He needed to take them from "here" to "there" in their faith—it's no different in our own lives. God wants to take us from "here," in our faith, and bring us "there"—a place of walking in greater faith for the journey ahead. When you take a journey with Jesus, it's like nothing you've ever experienced. It's simply not of this world. When you're walking with Jesus, you're taking a supernatural, spiritual, journey where He prepares you to live eternally.

Although we may not particularly like some of the paths on our journey . . . the destination of a closer relationship with God is worth all the storms we may have to endure. If you're following Jesus, you know where you're going—He's assured you of the destination. It's all about the journey getting there. He'll take you step by step because *He doesn't want you to miss a thing.*

I have refined you but not in the way silver is refined. Rather, I have refined you in the furnace of suffering. I will rescue you for my sake-yes, for my own sake! (Isaiah 48:10 NLT)

It is often asked, "Was this the miracle of God calming the storm in the Sea or the miracle of Jesus teaching us how to calm the storm inside of us?" Jesus knew His Disciples' hearts, just like He knows your heart and mine.

O Lord, you have examined my heart and know everything about me. You know when I sit down or stand up. You know my every thought when far away. You chart the path ahead of me and tell me where to stop and rest. Every moment you know where I am. You know what I am going to say even before I say it, Lord. You both precede and follow me. You place your hand of blessing on my head. (Psalm 139:2 NLT)

As God lovingly allows us to venture into the storms of our lives, He is always at work — drawing us closer and closer to Him while weaving all our paths into His purposes. If you're trusting in God, you can't just look at your circumstances and think that is all there is to it. They are a parallel to something deeper and more important concerning the spirit within you.

In the storms of our lives, God will show us that we have a deeper need. We need to develop the faith that glorifies Him. We must recognize that we are in the hands of a loving Father who has put us right where we need to be, in order to teach us His ways and His will.

The answers for the storms in our lives come through the still small voice of God saying, *"I will not let you go down. You have no reason to despair. Rest in My Word. I am with you always."* Through His Word, He assures us that He has everything under control, and there is no reason to fear. In the words of an old Hymn,

> *Day by day and with each passing moment,*
> *Strength I find to meet my trials here;*
> *Trusting in my Father's wise bestowment,*
> *I've no cause for worry or for fear.*

If we want to understand God's purpose in the storm, we must learn that God has allowed the storms in our lives out of love and wisdom. God designed life to be full of the unexpected, so that we will constantly be reminded that *we're not in control.*

Satan fills us with the lies that we are our own gods, we are in charge, we can plan, and we can direct our future; to the degree that God has given us free will . . . there is some truth to that. But, the devil distorts it and leads us to believe that we can control *everything.* As hard as we might try...*we can't.* Jesus himself reminded us:

I tell you the truth, the Son can do nothing by himself; (John 5:19 NIV)

Before Jesus' crucifixion, Pilate asked Jesus, *"Don't you realize I have the power either to free you or to crucify you?"* Jesus' answer was simple, revealing, and full of Truth . . ."*You would have no power over me if it were not given to you from above"* (John 19:11 NIV).

Regardless of what storm we're facing in life, we can never forget the simple truth: *God is in charge.* As difficult as it is for us to understand, God's will in our lives has far greater purposes than we can imagine; yet, all of them are designed for greater good. We must face the Truth that says God is *ultimately* in control.

In understanding God's ways, we cannot decide to heartily accept some Truths, yet readily discount others. We must accept God's ways and trust in them; it's a decision we make that isn't based upon our desires or emotions. We walk by faith in our loving God. Take a moment to really grasp the following truth in Romans 9: 15-19 (NIV):

For he says to Moses, "I will have mercy on whom I have mercy, and I will have compassion on whom I have compassion." It does not, therefore, depend on man's desire or effort, but on God's mercy. For the Scripture says to Pharaoh: "I raised you up for this very purpose, that I might display my power in you and that my name might be proclaimed in all the earth." Therefore God has mercy on whom he wants to have mercy, and he hardens whom he wants to harden. One of you will say to me: "Then why does God still blame us? For who resists his will?" But who are you, O man, to talk back to God? "Shall what is formed say to him who formed it, 'Why did you make me like this?' "Does not the potter have the right to make out of the same lump of clay some pottery for noble purposes and some for common use?"

Even though our storms may come filled with pain and suffering, we are to clearly understand that they come from a loving God . . . and we must praise Him . . . *in* the storm.

Should we accept only good things from the hand of God and never anything bad? (Job 2:10 NLT)

An unknown poet expressed the depths of God's work in and through us in this way:

When God wants to drill a man,
And thrill a man,
And skill a man;
When God wants to mold a man
To play the noblest part,
Then he yearns with all his heart
To create so great and bold a man
That all the world shall be amazed,
Watch his methods, watch his ways—
How he ruthlessly perfects
Whom he royally elects.
How he hammers him and hurts him,
And with mighty blows, converts him
Into trial shapes of clay
Which only God understands.
While his tortured heart is crying,
And he lifts beseeching hands.
How he bends but never breaks
When his good he undertakes.
How he uses Whom he chooses,
And with every purpose, fuses him,
By every act, induces him
To try his splendor out.

God knows what he's about.

(We need to fully grasp what this poet did, God is at work, He has a purpose, and *He knows what He's doing.*)

One of God's primary purposes for our storms that we *can* understand is: He wants to conform us into the likeness of Christ.

For those God foreknew he also predestined to be conformed to the likeness of his Son, that he might be the firstborn among many brothers. (Romans 8:29 NIV)

He is molding us, so that our character mirrors that of Jesus: the way He thinks, loves, and forgives. Through the process, He is teaching us to depend on His presence, instead of relying on our own strength. We are to draw *all* of our strength from Him.

> *I am the vine; you are the branches.*
> *If a man remains in me and I in him,*
> *he will bear much fruit;*
> *apart from me you can do nothing.*
> (John 15:5 NIV)

As God works on our character, He uses our suffering to teach us to keep focused upon Him. God's incredible love for us does not eliminate the pain, suffering, and heartache that we might go through; but, His Promises assure us that He is with us, and He is using it all for good (Romans 8:28).

Through it all, we learn to trust that no matter how devastating the storm might be . . . God is with us. And if we trust and obey Him, He will strengthen us and fill us with hope in the *midst* of the storm.

> *We do not know what to do,*
> *but our eyes are upon you.*
> (2 Chronicles 20:12 NIV)

You see, His presence is made perfect in your weakness; it is in your weakest moments where He will comfort you, strengthen you, and reassure you of His faithfulness. He wants you to know that He is not in your life to stop the storms from coming, but to take you through them. *He wants your faith.*

> *And it is impossible to please God without faith.*
> *Anyone who wants to come to him must believe*
> *that God exists and that he rewards*
> *those who sincerely seek him.*
> (Hebrews 11:6 NLT)

God's Presence in the Storm

We can be certain that God would never test our faith and then push us out to sea without His presence. The question is, "Do *you* acknowledge His presence during these storms of life?" The even greater question is, *"At what point* do you acknowledge His presence?" We storm the gates of heaven, wondering, *"Where is God?"* Yet, we fail to see that He is there with us . . . *and He's been there all along.* In fact, He's in the clouds — He's hovering over us each day, going before us, preparing a way through the storm.

The cloud of the Lord was over them by day when they set out from the camp. (Numbers 10:34 NIV)

They have heard that You, O Lord, are in the midst of this people, for You, O Lord, are seen eye to eye, while Your cloud stands over them; and You go before them in a pillar of cloud by day and in a pillar of fire by night. (Numbers 14:14 NASB)

Just think about the fact that the Disciples were in a boat, with who they supposedly believed was the Son of God; yet, even *they* failed to acknowledge Him, until it was almost too late. They were about to die! Why didn't it occur to them to ask for Jesus' help sooner? From the outside looking in, the answer seemed so obvious. In our own storms of life, it's often difficult to see the "obvious." Our vision becomes clouded with debilitating doubt and paralyzing fear.

The Disciples had seen Jesus perform many miracles — we have seen God work miracles in our own lives, yet we so easily forget them. Jesus says, *"Don't you remember?"*(Matthew 16:9) If they had faith in Him, the answer would be obvious — ask the Son of God to calm the storm! But they didn't. God knew that the Disciples' faith would grow through this experience. Their greater faith would enable them to be better witnesses. The miracles He performed were to teach us to have faith in Him, regardless of our circumstances — no matter how impossible things might seem. God reminds us through His Word:

Everything is possible for him who believes.
(Mark 9:23 NIV)

Have faith in God. (Mark 11:22 NIV)

The message God has for *you* is no different than it was for the Disciples. He wants you to know that faith in Him can bring about miracles in your life.

Many of us believe that miracles won't happen to us. Or maybe we're like the Disciples and we think that we have the ability to make it through this storm on our own. But, when we can't seem to rescue ourselves, we finally, as a last ditch effort, ask for God's help. Hear this truth: *"You don't have to save yourself."* (Besides, you can't!) Jesus came so that you don't have to . . . *He's the one who saves you through every storm of life.* He is all you need.

We tend to wait until the last moment because we seem to think that God can't possibly intervene in our situation. How much peace do we forfeit by struggling for the answers on our own? How much pain do we needlessly bear because we agonize over possibilities that never happen? We tend to believe that there are some things that God can handle, but we're convinced that on many things . . . *He needs our help.* At other times, we're certain that it's necessary for us to take control . . . God just seems to be taking too long. Even the Disciples, at some point, subconsciously believed that there was nothing that Jesus could do to help them calm the wind and waves of the storm. It was the perfect set up for the perfect miracle. ***God knows what He's doing.***

In the storm, He's bringing us to a place of embracing the truth that our life is better managed by

His hands, not our own. Trust Him—He does a much better job than we could ever do.

When miracles happen,
hope destroys hopelessness,
joy overcomes pain, love conquers hate,
and faith finds God in the midst of it all.

In the face of impossible circumstances, God says, "Lift up your eyes. Look beyond the visible realities." God doesn't work in the "natural." He works in the "*super*natural." His only requirement is that we no longer be "unbelieving," but "believing." He says, "*Believe and have faith that I am at work*, and I will enrich your life beyond your imagination." Do you dare believe God? When miracles happen, hope destroys hopelessness, joy overcomes pain, love conquers hate, and *faith finds God in the midst of it all* . . . ever present . . . worthy of praise.

Who doesn't want a miracle? Who doesn't want to be saved from the paralyzing grip of fear? We beg God for a miracle, but when He shows up, we're often found with very little faith—we're like the Disciples, standing in awe and amazement.

Our faith should never be surprised to see God's hand, when we've come to a place of surrender.

In our world, becoming mature means becoming "independent." In our spiritual journey, maturity means becoming *helplessly dependent upon God*. Our peace in the storm can only come from our resignation into God's hands. Regardless of how hopeless a situation might seem, we must surrender all of our hopes and expectations into His hands; when we do, we find that He will empower us to endure any hardship. His desire is that we would continue the journey without fear or anxiety, while trusting in His care. The more resigned we are to God's care, the less power our circumstances have over us. When we're resigned to God's care, we won't be frightened by undesirable news, and we won't be trying to constantly figure out the next step. If we have faith in God, we will simply trust, wait, and *expect* God.

Such people will not be overcome by evil. Those who are righteous will be long remembered. <u>They do not fear bad news; they confidently trust the Lord to care for them.</u> They are confident and fearless and can face their foes triumphantly. (Psalm 112:6-8 NLT)

Quite possibly, you're not sure that you want to take that step. You might feel that "trusting

God" comes with too much obligation. You might decide that you don't want to feel a burden of having to "repay" God for His miracle in your life. You may desire His hand, but you're not sure about coming face to face with Him (Job 23:15). You may be overwhelmed in feeling that you would be in debt to Him and you don't want to carry that weight. The truth is that you're already in deeper debt to Him than you'll ever imagine; that's why He sent Jesus. *Jesus can save you*. It's the storms of your life that bring you to a place of surrender. God wants you to stop all of your "trying" and simply start "trusting." He wants to eliminate the fleshly part of you that wants to control your life. He wants you to encounter something much more wonderful than anything you could devise. When you truly understand your storms of life, you will find that your storms will allow God to lift you up and give you true life to the full . . . *until it overflows*.

It's possible that if we never had to face our storms of life, we wouldn't seek the Lord. The purpose of your storm, simply put, is all about your relationship with Jesus. It's all out your faith in Him.

In John Ortberg's book, *"Faith and Doubt,"* he defines our faith and hope by saying that, *"Hope* points to one Man, one hope, one God who is worth trusting, not because of who He is. He is the one in whom and by whom we can hope." Faith looks Jesus in the eyes and says, "Yes Lord, wherever You lead . . . I will follow." We can trust that if He leads us into a raging storm, or allows a storm to come into our lives, He's got something amazing in mind. He wants to show you His sufficiency, His comforting presence, and His strength that will help you endure. Your *trials* become *tools* in the hand of God. Tell Him you'll follow Him — *then watch Him go to work.*

Then Jesus said to the Disciples,
"If any of you wants to be my follower,
you must put aside your selfish ambition,
shoulder your cross and follow me.
If you try to keep your life for yourself,
you will lose it.
But if you give up your life for me,
you will find true life."
(Mark 8:34-35 NLT)

When you bow down before the Lord
and admit your dependence on him,
he will lift you up and give you honor.
(James 4:10 NLT)

The Call of the Storm

Storms of life are used by God to strengthen your faith in Him. He's asking you to step out in faith and show Him that you are ready to live with Him forever. The storms call us to a higher place — they prove our faith and mature us spiritually. God may or may not have sent the storm into our life, but we can rest assured that He is with us through it all. The more we trust Him, the more our faith will grow. Placing our trust in Him will make all the difference for the journey.

Don't make the mistake of basing your faith on a particular outcome. We've all done it. We've prayed for God to answer our prayers with very detailed expectations, and we've seen our faith crumble to pieces when things didn't happen the way we thought they should. We find ourselves embracing "positive thinking," instead of real faith. Faith that grows us trusts in "Someone" rather than "something." Faith trusts in the character of God who is merciful, loving, and just. God doesn't ask us to "blindly" trust Him. He reveals Himself through Scripture and through our experiences to convince us that He *is* trustworthy.

The call of the storms in your life is to have greater faith in God. Your circumstances might look hopeless, you may have cried out to God for help, and you may have only heard a deafening silence; but, in your moments of abandoning all hope, you will find yourself in awe and amazement when you witness the power of God in your life. Your momentary pain and suffering will vanish, in an instant, when you open your soul to the risks of faith. Faith in God will bring you to the edge . . . *every time*. Each step of faith will demand that you reach out for the hand of God. He wants you to be a witness to His awesome presence and power.

The call of the storm in the Disciples' lives caused them to be devoted witnesses to Christ because they experienced a "personal" miracle through the magnificent power of God—Jesus calmed their storm . . . He saved their lives.

Then Jesus told him, "You believe because you have
seen me. Blessed are those who haven't seen
me and believe anyway."
(John 20:29 NLT)

When trying to understand how this miracle relates to your life and the storms you face, it is important to realize that the storm did not slowly subside or die down—when the Disciples cried out to Jesus for help . . . it stopped immediately! It appears that from that moment on, the Disciples were overwhelmed, not only with the power that Jesus possessed, but that He truly must be the Son of God. When the Disciples witnessed this great miracle, they were suddenly overcome by its "stillness." Imagine being more frightened of how your storm of life is "stilled," rather than of the fear of the raging storm itself!

Behind every storm there is a blessing.
View your storm as a revelation from God,
an opportunity to learn to trust Him,
and a stepping stone
for better things in the future.

Can you imagine? Whatever storm you're currently in, God can stop it *immediately.*

When we call upon the name of Jesus, He does hear us; He will answer us through the storm. Will you call upon Him now? Will you show Him your faith in Him and cry out to Him even when you cannot see Him? *Or will you keep trying to bail water out of a boat that is already capsizing?*

The Disciples were truly the closest men to the Son of God; yet, at the end of this miracle we see that *even they* had doubts in their heart about who Jesus really was. They saw with their own eyes all of the miracles He performed, but they still asked, *"Who is this man?"* A little surprising . . . don't you think? Onlookers may have believed that the Disciples must have had the highest level of faith — they left their lives and followed Jesus. But, Jesus knew where their faith was lacking. Jesus saw their hearts . . . just like He sees yours. You cannot hide your heart from God.

It is in our storms where the areas of our lives that are hindering our spiritual growth are revealed. It is in the storms that God will reveal, refine, strengthen, and perfect those areas . . . if you allow Him to take you through the storm.

You can trust God. He already knows exactly what He's going to do in your situation. He has a plan. He wants you to place your trust in Him by saying, *"You are God, and nothing is impossible with You. I am giving this situation to You and it is no longer mine but yours to deal with as You will. "*He's taking your faith to a place of understanding His desire and ability to work a miracle for you — not only in your current storm, but in every storm you will ever face. His desire is that you would develop an unwavering faith that is *anchored* in Him.

Trust in, lean on, rely on, and have confidence
in Him at all times, you people; pour out your hearts
before Him. God is a refuge for us (a fortress and a high
tower). Selah [pause, and calmly think of that]!
(Psalm 62:8 AMP)

The Blessing Behind the Storm

It should be comforting to know that although God allows the storm, Jesus is in the boat with you. Yes, He is with you, right now, in the boat where you sit in the midst of your storm. The difference is: He is in the stern resting because He knows the blessing behind all of the wind and rain. He knows that the destruction in your life can be used to rebuild your life and make it better than it was before. He knows that God has the power to turn your ashes to beauty.

To all who mourn in Israel, he will give beauty for ashes, joy instead of mourning, praise instead of despair. For the Lord has planted them strong and graceful oaks for his own glory. (Isaiah 61:3 NLT)

There is no storm that is not permitted and controlled by God. When Jesus rose from the dead, He overcame every spirit in opposition to Him. By His resurrection, Jesus proclaimed power over all demonic forces in your life. This means that whatever your storm is, God has allowed it, and it has been overcome through Christ — just knowing this should bring about a great blessing in your spirit. Behind every storm there is a blessing — God has assured us there is one. Why not view this time as a revelation from God, an opportunity to learn to trust Him, and a stepping stone to better things in the future. He's assured us:

God blesses the people who patiently endure testing.
(James 1:12 NLT)

For the Disciples, their blessing was acquiring greater faith in God which made them the greatest witnesses for Christ — what a blessing for you and I! When God allows a storm in your life . . . it has great purpose; if you miss the purpose, you may miss God's will for your life.

Every intimate part of our lives is no surprise to God. Many times, when He leads us into the storms, He's leading us to a place of surrender and complete dependence upon Him. The storms aren't necessarily to show us His incredible powers; although His love, mercy, and grace continually amaze even those with incredible faith. God doesn't have to prove His power, just as He doesn't have to prove His existence—it's the obvious. We just have to open our eyes and look around us. We don't have to go very far to realize there is an amazing God who keeps the world in motion, and He has addressed every intricate detail which sustains life here on earth.

God is more interested in showing us the heart of who He is. God wants us to understand that our storms are more than just storms. They are more than just the pain and suffering on the surface. Our storms build a bridge to an intimate relationship with Him. The storms just give God another opportunity to demonstrate His unconditional love for us.

He wants you to understand, firsthand, what it feels like to reach out and have His hand grasp yours. He wants you to understand what it's like to see His face and hear His voice. No one and nothing can simply give you this intimate understanding through witnessing. Others' relationship with God can you *lead* you to Him, but He does the rest. God wants a very personal relationship with you . . . He wants you to experience a miracle *in your own life*. The Disciples had witnessed many miracles that Jesus had performed, yet they had not experienced a miracle for themselves; when Jesus calmed the storm, they were given a "personal" miracle.

God wants to give you greater knowledge of Himself, so that when the storms rage around you, you can have peace because you have learned that He is in control and there is nothing to fear. He wants you to be assured that He is with you, He will carry you, and He is your refuge and source of strength.

You can rest assured through God's Promises that He will use every storm for your good and His greater purposes.
God always has a plan. Trust Him —
get to the back of the boat with Jesus.

God is our refuge and strength, always ready to help in times of trouble. (Psalm 46:1 NLT)

When you understand your storms and grasp the fact that Jesus is in your boat, you, too, can experience a miracle in your storm. When you seek out God's call to you through the storm, allowing Him to use it all for His purposes, your storms will bring about great blessings in your life. You'll even find that your storms of life will be used by God to bless the lives of others! You can rest assured through God's Promises . . . He will use *every* storm for your good and His greater purposes. God always as a plan. Trust Him. It's your life He wants to use, but He can't use you unless you're in the *back* of the boat with Jesus—at rest, trusting Him. So, the begging question is:

"Where are you in the boat right now?"

Scriptures to Encourage You in the Storm

These trials are only to test your faith, to show that it is strong and pure. It is being tested as fire tests and purifies gold — and your faith is far more precious to God than mere gold. So if your faith remains strong after being tried by fiery trials, it will bring you much praise and glory and honor on the day when Jesus Christ is revealed to the whole world. (1 Peter 1:7 NLT)

So, be truly glad! There is wonderful joy ahead, even though it is necessary for you to endure many trials for a while. (1 Peter 1:6 NLT)

I know the Lord is always with me. I will not be shaken, for he is right beside me. (Psalm 16:8 NLT)

So be strong and take courage, all you who put your hope in the Lord! (Psalm 31:24 NLT)

"For I know the plans I have for you," says the Lord. "They are plans for good and not for disaster, to give you a future and a hope. In those days when you pray, I will listen. If you look for me in earnest, you will find me when you seek me." (Jeremiah 29:11 NLT)

Draw close to God, and God will draw close to you. (James 4:8 NLT)

We can rejoice, too, when we run into problems and trials, for we know that they are good for us — they help us learn strength of character in us, and character strengthens our confident expectations of salvation. And this expectation will not disappoint us for we know how dearly God loves us, because he has given us the Holy Spirit to fill our hearts with his love. (Romans 5:3 NLT)

So let us come boldly to the throne of our gracious God. There we will receive his mercy, and we will find grace to help us when we need it. (Hebrews 4:16 NLT)

God is our refuge and strength, always ready to help in times of trouble. (Psalm 46:1 NLT)

I have refined you but not in the way silver is refined. Rather, I have refined you in the furnace of suffering. I will rescue you for my sake, — yes, for my own sake! (Isaiah 48:10 NLT)

We are pressed on every side by troubles, but we are not crushed and broken. We are perplexed, but we don't give up and quit. We are hunted down, but God never abandons us. We get knocked down, but we get up again and keep going… (2 Corinthians 4: 8-10 NLT)

For you will rescue me from my troubles and help me to triumph . . . (Psalm 54:7 NLT)

So humble yourselves under the mighty power of God, and in his good time he will honor you. Give all your worries and cares to God, for he cares about what happens to you. (1 Peter 5:6-7 NLT)

Do not fear anything except the Lord Almighty. He alone is the Holy one. If you fear him, you need fear nothing else. He will keep you safe.
(Isaiah 8: 12-14 NLT)

In quietness and in trusting confidence I find strength.
(Isaiah 30:15 NLT)

It was by faith that Moses left the land of Egypt, not fearing the king's anger. He kept right on going because he kept his eyes on the one who is invisible.
(Hebrews 11:27-28 NLT)

We do not know what to do, but our eyes are upon you.
(2 Chronicles 20:12 NLT)

In quietness and confidence is your strength.
(Isaiah 30:15 NLT)

About the Author

*Cherie Hill is the founder of ScriptureNow.com
Ministry which brings the Word of God
into over 30 countries around the world.
She has a BA in Psychology and is trained in Biblical
Counseling through the AACC.
She is an Amazon.com Bestselling Christian Living
Author, ranked among the top 10 authors for Religion and
Spirituality, who spends her time at the feet of Jesus.*

Bestselling Author of:

WAITING on GOD

Hope Being Gone

empty.
(Living Full of Faith When Life Drains You Dry)

BE STILL
(Let Jesus Calm Your Storms)

Beginning at The End
(Finding God When Your World Falls Apart)

THE WAYS of GOD
(Finding Purpose Through Your Pain)

Made in the USA
Las Vegas, NV
19 March 2021

19830947R00115